Windows PowerShell

Fast Start

2nd Edition

Your Quick Start Guide for Windows PowerShell.

Smart Brain Training Solutions

Thank you for purchasing *Windows PowerShell Fast Start*! We hope you'll look for our other *Fast Start* guides.

Table of Contents

1. Getting Started with Windows PowerShell

Windows PowerShell provides a full-featured command shell built on a programming language. Not unlike the less sophisticated Windows command prompt, PowerShell operates by executing built-in commands, external commands, and command-line utilities and then returning the results in an output stream as text. The output stream can be manipulated in various ways, including redirecting it so that it can be used as input for another command. The process of redirecting one command's output to another command's input is called *piping*, and it is a widely used scripting technique.

PowerShell implements a scripting language based on C# and an object model based on the Microsoft .NET Framework. Basing the scripting language for Windows PowerShell on C# ensures that the scripting language can be easily understood by current C# developers and also allows new developers to advance to C#. Using an object model based on the .NET Framework allows Windows PowerShell to pass complete objects and all their properties as output from one command to another.

The ability to redirect objects is extremely powerful and allows for a dynamic manipulation of result sets. For example, you can get not only the name of a particular user but also the entire related user object. You can then manipulate the properties of this user object by referring to the properties you want to work with by name.

Windows and Windows Server operating systems are released with a specific version of Windows PowerShell:

- Windows PowerShell 5.0 is built into Windows 10 and Windows Server 2016. Also, you can install PowerShell 5.0 on computers running earlier releases by installing Windows Management Framework 5.0.
- Windows PowerShell 4.0 is built into Windows 8.1 and Windows Server 2012 Release 2 (R2). Also, you can install PowerShell 4.0 on computers running Windows 7 with Service Pack 1 or later, and Windows Server 2008 R2 with Service Pack 1 or later by installing Windows Management Framework 4.0.
- Windows PowerShell 3.0 is built into Windows 8 and Windows Server 2012. Also, you can install PowerShell 3.0 on computers running Windows 7 with Service Pack 1 or later, Windows Server 2008 R2 with Service Pack 1 or later, and Windows Server 2008 with Service Pack 2 or later by installing Windows Management Framework 3.0.

The prerequisites for using Windows PowerShell depend on the version you are working with. Generally, you must install the appropriate version of the Microsoft .NET Framework. You must also ensure WS-Management and Windows Management Instrumentation (WMI) are available. WS-Management supports the Windows Remote Management (WinRM) service and the WS-Management (WSMan) protocol. Windows Management Instrumentation which supports PowerShell features that access managed resources through WMI.

REAL WORLD   The Distributed Management Task Force (DMTF) created the Common Information Model (CIM) standard to describe the structure and behavior of managed resources. Windows Management Instrumentation (WMI) is a CIM server service that implements the CIM standard on Windows.

> WS-Management (WS-Man) is a protocol for managing
> communications between a CIM client and a CIM server. WS-
> Man is based on Simple Object Access Protocol (SOAP),
> which is implemented using the eXtensible Markup
> Language (XML).
>
> Windows Remote Management (WinRM) is the Microsoft
> implementation of the WS-Man protocol on Windows.

These components are included in Windows 8, Windows 8.1,
Windows 10, Windows Server 2012, Windows Server 2012 R2,
and Windows Server 2016. For other supported operating
systems, these components are installed when you install
Windows Management Framework as required. Different builds
are available for each version of Windows, in 32-bit and 64-bit
editions.

Working with the Windows PowerShell Console

Windows PowerShell has both a command-line environment
and a graphical environment for running commands and scripts.
The PowerShell console (powershell.exe) is a 32-bit or 64-bit
environment for working with PowerShell at the command line.
On 32-bit versions of Windows, you'll find the 32-bit executable
in the %SystemRoot%\System32\WindowsPowerShell\v1.0
directory. On 64-bit versions of Windows, you'll find the 32-bit
executable in the %SystemRoot%\SysWow64\Windows
PowerShell\v1.0 directory and the 64-bit executable in the
%SystemRoot%\System32\WindowsPowerShell\v1.0 directory.

> **NOTE** %SystemRoot% refers to the SystemRoot
> environment variable. The Windows operating system has
> many environment variables, which are used to refer to user-

specific and system-specific values. I'll often refer to environment variables using the standard Windows syntax %VariableName%. In Windows PowerShell, you access and work with environment variables using the Env provider.

The Standard Console

With Windows 7, Windows Server 2008 and Windows Server 2008 R2, you can start the PowerShell console by using the Search box on the Start menu. Click Start, type **powershell** in the Search box, and then press Enter. Or, you can click Start, point to All Programs, point to Accessories, Windows PowerShell, and then choose Windows PowerShell.

If you are working with a later versions of Windows, you can start the PowerShell console by using the Search box. Type **powershell** in the Search box, and then press Enter. Or you can click Start, click the All Apps button, and then choose Windows PowerShell.

Regardless of which version of Windows you are using, the 64-bit version of the PowerShell console is started by default on 64-bit systems. If you want to use the 32-bit PowerShell console on a 64-bit system, you must select the Windows PowerShell (x86) option.

You can start Windows PowerShell from a Windows command shell (cmd.exe) by entering the following:

```
powershell
```

The Elevated, Administrator Console

The standard Windows PowerShell console runs with no security context and you won't be able to perform administrative tasks. To change computer settings and perform other administrative tasks, you'll need to run the PowerShell console in elevated, administrator mode.

With Windows 7, Windows Server 2008 and Windows Server 2008 R2, you can run the PowerShell console in elevated, administrator mode by using the Search box on the Start menu. Click Start, type **powershell** in the Search box, right-click Windows PowerShell in the search results and then select Run As Administrator. Or, you can click Start, point to All Programs, point to Accessories, Windows PowerShell. Next, right-click the Windows PowerShell menu item and then select Run As Administrator.

If you are working with a later versions of Windows, you can run the PowerShell console in elevated, administrator mode by using the Search box. Type **powershell** in the Search box, right-click Windows PowerShell in the search results and then select Run As Administrator.

> **REAL WORLD**   By default with Windows 8.1, Windows 10, Windows Server 2012 R2, and Windows Server 2016, Command Prompt and Command Prompt (Admin) are options on the shortcut menu that is displayed when you right-click in the lower left corner or press Windows key + X. The alternative is for the Windows PowerShell prompt and the Windows PowerShell (Admin) prompt to be displayed on this menu. To configure which options are available, on the desktop, right-click the taskbar and then select Properties. In

the Taskbar And Navigation Properties dialog box, on the Navigation tab, select or clear the Replace Command Prompt With Windows PowerShell... checkbox as appropriate.

You can start an elevated, administrator Windows PowerShell console from an elevated, administrator command shell (cmd.exe) by entering the following:

```
powershell
```

The PowerShell Console

Figure 1 shows a PowerShell window. By default, the window is 120 characters wide and displays 50 lines of text. When additional text is to be displayed in the window or you enter commands and the PowerShell console's window is full, the current text is displayed in the window, and prior text is scrolled up. If you want to pause the display temporarily when a command is writing output, press Ctrl+S. Afterward, press Ctrl+S to resume or Ctrl+C to terminate execution.

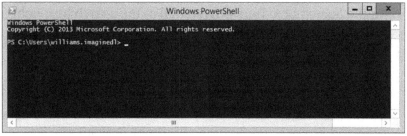

FIGURE 1 When you work with PowerShell, you'll frequently use the command-line environment.

In this figure, the display text is:

```
Windows PowerShell
```

```
Copyright (c) 2013 Microsoft Corporation. All rights
reserved.

PS C:\Users\williams.imagined1>
```

Here, the command prompt for the PowerShell shows the
current working directory preceded by PS. A blinking cursor
following the command prompt indicates that PowerShell is in
interactive processing mode. In interactive mode, you can type
commands directly after the prompt and press Enter to execute
them. For example, type **get-childitem** and then press Enter to
get a listing of the current directory.

> **NOTE** When working with a standard PowerShell window,
> the default path is based on the current value of
> %UserProfile%, meaning the user profile directory for the
> current user. When you run PowerShell in elevated,
> administrator mode, the default path is %WinDir%\System32,
> meaning the System32 directory for the Windows
> installation.
>
> **MORE INFO** Get-ChildItem is used to get items in specified
> locations. Get-ChildItem works with the filesystem by default,
> but can be used with other data providers, such as the Env
> provider or the Cert provider, which are used to work with
> environment variables and digital certificates respectively. For
> example, you can list all environment variables on a
> computer by entering **get-childitem env:**.

Windows PowerShell also has a noninteractive processing
mode, which is used when executing a series of commands. In
noninteractive processing mode, PowerShell reads and executes
commands one by one but doesn't present a prompt to the
user. Typically, commands are read from a script file, but you

can start the PowerShell console in noninteractive processing mode.

To exit PowerShell, type **exit**. If you started PowerShell from a command prompt, typing **exit** will return you to the command prompt. If you want to run a separate instance of PowerShell from within PowerShell, you also can type **powershell** at the PowerShell prompt. Invoking PowerShell in this way allows you to use a separate session and initialize PowerShell with specific parameters.

Working with the Windows PowerShell ISE

The official name of the graphical environment for Windows PowerShell is the Windows PowerShell Integrated Scripting Environment (ISE). Using the PowerShell application (powershell_ise.exe), you can run commands and write, run, and debug scripts in a single integrated interface. There are 32-bit and 64-bit graphical environments for working with PowerShell, and you'll find the related executables in the same location as the PowerShell console.

With Windows 7, Windows Server 2008 and Windows Server 2008 R2, you can start the PowerShell application by using the Search box on the Start menu. Click Start, type **powershell** in the Search box, and then press Enter. Or, you can click Start, point to All Programs, point to Accessories, Windows PowerShell, and then choose Windows PowerShell ISE. Or, right-click the Windows PowerShell ISE menu item and then select Run As Administrator to run the PowerShell application in elevated, administrator mode.

If you are working with a later versions of Windows, you can start the PowerShell application by using the Apps Search box. Type **powershell** in the Apps Search box, and then choose Windows PowerShell ISE. Or you can click the Windows logo, click the Apps button and then choose Windows PowerShell ISE. Or, right-click Windows PowerShell ISE and then select Run As Administrator to run the PowerShell application in elevated, administrator mode.

Regardless of which version of Windows you are using, the 64-bit version of the PowerShell ISE is started by default on 64-bit systems. If you want to use the 32-bit application on a 64-bit system, you must select the Windows PowerShell ISE (x86) option.

You can start the PowerShell application from a command prompt (cmd.exe) by entering:

```
powershell_ise
```

Figure 2 shows the main window for the PowerShell application. Here, the main window displays the Script pane and the Console pane. In the Script pane, you can type the commands and text for PowerShell scripts. In the Console pane, you can enter commands at a prompt as you would using the PowerShell console and display the results of running scripts or commands.

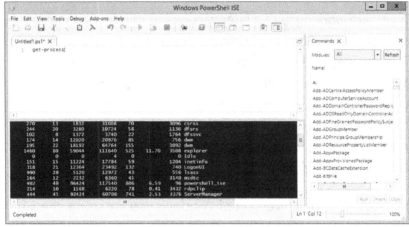

FIGURE 2 Use the PowerShell ISE when you are creating scripts.

As you enter text into the Script pane, the text is color coded depending on whether it is a cmdlet, function, variable, or other type of text. To run your script and display the related output in the Console pane, click the Run Script button on the toolbar or press F5. To run part of a script, select the commands to run in the Script pane and then select Run Selection or press F8.

After you enter the text of your script, you can save the script with the .ps1 extension. Click the Save option on the toolbar or press Ctrl+S. In the Save As dialog box, choose a save location, enter a name for the script and then click Save. See "Understanding Scripts & Script Execution" in Chapter 2 later in this text for more information on working with scripts.

Options on the View menu allow you to control the display and location of the Script pane. Select Show Script Pane to display the Script pane if it is hidden. Select the option again to hide the Script pane if it is displayed. When the Script pane is displayed, you can select Script Pane Right to display the Script pane on the right rather than at the top of the main window.

Select the option again to restore the original position. You can resize the panes by clicking and dragging as well.

The default text size is fairly small. You can change the text size by using the Zoom slider in the lower-right corner of the main window. Alternatively, press Ctrl and+ to increase the text size, or press Ctrl and – to decrease the text size.

To exit the PowerShell application, press Alt+F4 or select the Exit option on the File menu. You can also exit by typing **exit** at the PowerShell prompt in the Console pane.

Managing Windows PowerShell Console Properties

If you use the Windows PowerShell console frequently, you'll definitely want to customize its properties. For example, you can add buffers so that text scrolled out of the viewing area is accessible. You can resize the console, change its fonts, and more.

To get started, click the PowerShell prompt icon at the top of the console window or right-click the console's title bar and then select Properties. As Figure 3 shows, the Properties dialog box has four tabs:

 ▪ **Options**   Allows you to configure cursor size, edit options, and command history. Select QuickEdit Mode if you want to use a single mouse click to paste copied text into the PowerShell window. Clear QuickEdit Mode if you want to right-click and then select Paste to insert copied text. Clear Insert Mode to overwrite text as the default editing mode. Use the command history to configure how previously used commands are buffered in memory. (You'll find more information about the command history in the next section of this text, "Using the Command History.")

- **Font** Allows you to set the font size and face used by the PowerShell prompt. Raster font sizes are set according to their pixel width and height. For example, the size 8 × 12 is 8 screen pixels wide and 12 screen pixels high. Other fonts are set by point size, such as 10-point Lucida Console. Interestingly, when you select a point size of n, the font will be n pixels high; therefore, a 10-point font is 10 screen pixels high. These fonts can be designated as a bold font type as well, which increases their screen pixel width.

- **Layout** Allows you to set the screen buffer size, window size, and window position. Size the buffer height so that you can easily scroll back through previous listings and script output. A good setting is in the range of 2,000 to 3,000. Size the window height so that you can view more of the PowerShell window at one time. A good setting is a width of 120 and a height of 60. If you want the PowerShell window to be in a specific screen position when started, clear Let System Position Window and then specify a position, in pixels, for the upper-left corner of the PowerShell window by using Left and Top.

- **Colors** Allows you to set the text and background colors used by the PowerShell console. Screen Text and Screen Background control the respective color settings for the window. The Popup Text and Popup Background options control the respective color settings for any pop-up dialog boxes generated when running commands at the PowerShell prompt.

FIGURE 3 Configure PowerShell console properties for your environment.

When you are finished updating the window properties, click OK to save your settings to your user profile. Your settings modify only the shortcut that started the current window. Any time you start PowerShell using the applicable shortcut, PowerShell will use these settings. If, however, you start PowerShell using a different shortcut, you'll have the settings associated with that shortcut.

Using the Command History

The command history buffer is a feature of Windows PowerShell that stores commands you've used in the current session and allows you to access them without having to retype the command text. The maximum number of commands to buffer is set through the PowerShell Properties dialog box discussed in the previous section. By default, up to 50 commands are stored.

You can change the history size by completing these steps:

1. Right-click the PowerShell console's title bar, select Properties, and then click the Options tab.

2. Use the Buffer Size field to set the maximum number of commands to store in the history, and then click OK to save your settings to your user profile.

Your settings modify only the shortcut that started the current window. Any time you start a PowerShell using the applicable shortcut, it will use these settings. If, however, you start a PowerShell using a different shortcut, you'll have the settings associated with that shortcut.

You can access commands stored in the history in the following ways:

- **Browsing with the arrow keys**   Use the up arrow and down arrow keys to move up and down through the list of buffered commands. When you find the command you want to use, press Enter to execute it as entered previously, or you can modify the command text displayed by adding or changing parameters and then pressing Enter.

- **Browsing the command history pop-up window** Press F7 to display a pop-up window that contains a listing of buffered commands. Next, select a command using the arrow keys. (Alternatively, press F9, press the corresponding number on the keyboard, and then press Enter.) Execute the selected command by pressing Enter, or press Esc to close the pop-up window without executing a command.
- **Searching the command history** Enter the first few letters of the command you want to execute, and then press F8. PowerShell searches through the history for the first command that begins with the characters you entered. Press Enter to execute it, or press F8 again to search the history buffer for the next match in the command history.

As you work with the command history, keep in mind that each instance of Windows PowerShell has its own set of command buffers. Thus, buffers are valid only in the related PowerShell context.

2. Managing Cmdlets and Scripts

Windows PowerShell introduces the concept of a cmdlet (pronounced *commandlet*). A cmdlet is the smallest unit of functionality in Windows PowerShell. You can think of a cmdlet as a built-in command. Rather than being highly complex, most cmdlets are quite simple and have a small set of associated properties.

Working with Cmdlets

You use cmdlets the same way you use any other commands and utilities. Cmdlet names are not case sensitive. This means you can use a combination of both uppercase and lowercase characters. After starting Windows PowerShell, you can enter the name of the cmdlet at the prompt, and it will run in much the same way as a command-line command.

Understanding Cmdlet Names

For ease of reference, cmdlets are named using verb-noun pairs. As Table 1 shows, the verb tells you what the cmdlet does in general. The noun tells you what specifically the cmdlet works with. Verbs and nouns are always separated by a hyphen with no spaces. For example, the Get-Variable cmdlet gets a named Windows PowerShell variable and returns its value. If you don't specify which variable to get as a parameter, Get-Variable returns a list of all PowerShell variables and their values. You also can get a list of all PowerShell variables and their values by entering **get-childitem variable:**.

TABLE 1 Common Verbs Used with Cmdlets

CMDLET VERB	USAGE
Add	Adds an instance of an item, such as a history entry or snap-in.
Clear	Removes the contents of an item, such as an event log or variable value.
ConvertFrom	Converts an item from one format to another, such as converting from a list of comma-separated values to object properties.
ConvertTo	Converts an item to a particular format, such as converting object properties to a list of comma-separated values.
Disable	Disables an enabled setting, such as disabling remote connections.
Enable	Enables a disabled setting, such as enabling remote connections.
Export	Exports an item's properties in a particular format, such as exporting console properties in XML format.
Get	Queries a specific object or a subset of a type of object, such as getting a list of running processes.
Import	Imports an item's properties from a particular format, such as importing console properties from serialized XML.

Invoke	Executes an instance of an item, such as an expression.
New	Creates a new instance of an item, such as a new variable or event.
Remove	Removes an instance of an item, such as a variable or event.
Set	Modifies specific settings of an object.
Start	Starts an instance of an item, such as a service or process.
Stop	Stops an instance of an item, such as a service or process.
Test	Tests an instance of an item for a specific state or value, such as testing a connection to see if it is valid
Write	Performs a write operation on an instance of an item, such as writing an event to the system event log.

Table 2 provides a list of basic utility cmdlets. Although many other cmdlets are available, these are the ones you're likely to use for performing basic tasks, such as comparing objects or getting account credentials.

TABLE 2 Basic Utility Cmdlets

CMDLET NAME	DESCRIPTION
Compare-Object, Group-Object, Sort-Object, Select-Object, New-Object	Cmdlets for comparing, grouping, sorting, selecting, and creating objects.
ConvertFrom-SecureString, ConvertTo-SecureString	Cmdlets for creating or exporting secure strings.
Get-Alias, New-Alias, Set-Alias, Export-Alias, Import-Alias	Cmdlets for getting, creating, setting, exporting, and importing aliases.
Get-Command, Invoke-Command, Measure-Command, Trace-Command	Cmdlets for getting information about cmdlets, invoking commands, measuring the run time of commands, and tracing commands.
Get-Credential	Gets a credential object based on a password.
Get-Date, Set-Date	Gets or sets the current date and time.
Get-ExecutionPolicy, Set-ExecutionPolicy	Gets or sets the effective execution policy for the current shell.
Get-Host	Gets information about the PowerShell host application.
Get-Location, Set-Location	Displays or sets the current working location.
Get-Process, Start-Process, Stop-Process	Gets, starts, or stops processes on a computer.

CMDLET NAME	DESCRIPTION
Get-PSDrive, New-PSDrive, Remove-PSDrive	Gets, creates, or removes a specified PowerShell drive.
Get-Service, New-Service, Set-Service	Gets, creates, or sets system services.
Get-Variable, New-Variable, Set-Variable, Remove-Variable, Clear-Variable	Cmdlets for getting, creating, setting, and removing variables as well as for clearing variable values.
Pop-Location	Obtains a pushed location from the stack.
Push-Location	Pushes a location to the stack
Read-Host, Write-Host, Clear-Host	Reads input from, writes output to, or clears the host window.
Start-Sleep	Suspends shell or script activity for the specified period.
Wait-Process	Waits for a process to be stopped before accepting input.
Write-Output	Writes an object to the pipeline.
Write-Warning	Displays a warning message.

You can work with cmdlets by executing them directly at the PowerShell prompt or by running commands from within scripts. The cmdlets available on a particular computer depend on the PowerShell modules that are installed. You can get information about installed modules using Get-Module. For example, if you enter **get-module –listavailable**, you can get a list of all installed modules.

You can get a complete list of cmdlets available by entering **get-command**. However, the output lists both cmdlets and functions by name and definition. With cmdlets, the definition provided is the syntax, but the full syntax rarely fits on the line. More often, you simply want to know if a cmdlet exists. You can display a formatted list of cmdlets by entering the following command:

```
get-command | format-wide -column 3
```

This command shows many of the features of PowerShell that you'll use regularly at the command line. The | symbol is called a pipe. Here, you pipe the output of Get-Command to Format-Wide. Format-Wide takes the output and formats it in multiple columns. The default number of columns is two, but here we used the Column parameter to specify that we wanted to format the output into three columns, as shown in this example:

```
A:                   Add-Computer         Add-Content
Add-History          Add-Member           Add-PSSnapin
Add-Type             B:                   C:
cd..                 cd\                  Checkpoint-Computer
Clear-Content        Clear-EventLog       Clear-History
Clear-Host           Clear-Item           Clear-ItemProperty
Clear-Variable       Compare-Object       Complete-Transaction
```

```
Connect-WSMan    ConvertFrom-Csv  ConvertFrom-
SecureString
```

A better way to get information about cmdlets is to use Get-Help. To get help for a particular cmdlet, you enter Get-Help followed by the cmdlet name, such as Get-Help Clear-History. If you enter **get-help *-***, you get a list of all cmdlets, which includes a synopsis that summarizes the purpose of the cmdlet—much more useful than a list of commands.

Rather than list all commands, you can list specific commands by name or by using wildcards. For example, if you know the command you are looking for begins with Get, enter **get-help get*** to view all commands that start with Get. If you know the command includes the word *computer*, you could enter **get-help *computer*** to view all commands that included this keyword. Finally, if you are looking for related commands on a specific subject, such as aliases, enter **get-help *** and then the keyword, such as **get-command *alias**.

As discussed later in the text in Chapter 3, "Using the Help Documentation," help files aren't included with the standard installation and Windows PowerShell displays automatically generated help information by default. However, when help files are available, you can examine cmdlet syntax and usage. Windows PowerShell provides three levels of Help documentation: standard, detailed, and full. If you want to view the standard Help documentation for a specific cmdlet, type **get-help** followed by the cmdlet name, such as:

```
get-help new-variable
```

The standard Help documentation provides the complete syntax for using a cmdlet, which includes details on any parameters the cmdlet supports and examples. By adding the –Detailed parameter, you can get detailed information about a cmdlet. Or you can get full technical information about a cmdlet by adding the –Full parameter. The detailed and the full documentation are both useful when you want to dig deeper, and usually either one will give you the information you are looking for.

When you work with cmdlets, you'll encounter two standard types of errors:

- **Terminating errors**   Errors that halt execution
- **Nonterminating errors**   Errors that cause error output to be returned but do not halt execution

With both types of errors, you'll typically see error text that can help you resolve the problem that caused it. For example, an expected file might be missing or you may not have sufficient permissions to perform a specified task.

Understanding Cmdlet Parameters

All cmdlet parameters are designated with an initial dash (–), such as –Name or –SourcePath. To reduce the amount of typing required, some parameters are position sensitive, so that you can sometimes pass parameters in a specific order without having to specify the parameter name. For example, in the syntax for the Get-Service cmdlet, you know the –Name parameter can be omitted because it is enclosed in brackets as shown here:

```
Get-Service [[-Name] Strings] [-ComputerName Strings]
```

```
[-DependentServices]  [-Include Strings]  [-Exclude
Strings]  [-RequiredServices]
```

Therefore, with Get-Service, you don't have to specify the –
Name parameter; you can simply type the following:

```
get-service ServiceName
```

where *ServiceName* is the name of the service you want to
examine, such as:

```
get-service winrm
```

This command line returns the status of the Windows Remote
Management service. Because you can use wildcards, such as *,
with name values, you can also type **get-service win*** to return
the status of all services whose names begin with *win*. Typically,
these will include the Windows Management Instrumentation
and Windows Remote Management services, as shown in this
example:

```
Status    Name                DisplayName
------    ----                -----------
Stopped   WinHttpAutoProx...  WinHTTP Web Proxy Auto-
Discovery
Running   Winmgmt             Windows Management
Instrumentation
Stopped   WinRM               Windows Remote Management
```

All cmdlets support a common set of parameters. Most cmdlets
that make changes support the risk mitigation parameters:
–Confirm and –WhatIf. A list of the common and risk mitigation
parameters is shown in Table 3. Although you can use the
common parameters with any cmdlet, they don't necessarily
have an effect with all cmdlets. For example, if a cmdlet doesn't

generate verbose output, using the –Verbose parameter has no effect.

TABLE 3 Common and Risk Mitigation Parameters

PARAMETER NAME	DESCRIPTION
–Confirm	Pauses execution and requires the user to acknowledge the action before continuing.
–Debug	Provides programming-level debugging information about the operation.
–ErrorAction	Controls the command behavior when an error occurs. Valid values are SilentlyContinue (suppress the error and continue), Continue (display the error and continue), Inquire (display the error and prompt to confirm before continuing), Suspend (suspends a workflow and only valid for workflows), and Stop (display the error and halt execution). The default value is Continue.
–ErrorVariable	Sets the name of the variable (in addition to the standard error) in which to store errors that have occurred.
–OutBuffer	Sets the output buffer for the cmdlet.
–OutVariable	Sets the name of the variable in which to place output objects.
-PipelineVariable	Saves the results or a piped command or part of a piped command that can be passed through the pipeline.

PARAMETER NAME	DESCRIPTION
–Verbose	Provides detailed information about the operation.
–WarningAction	Determines how a cmdlet responds to a warning message. Valid values are SilentlyContinue (suppress the warning and continue), Continue (display the warning and continue), Inquire (display the warning and prompt to confirm before continuing), and Stop (display the warning and halt execution). The default value is Continue.
–WarningVariable	Sets the name of the variable (in addition to the standard error) in which to store warnings that have occurred.
–WhatIf	Allows the user to view what would happen if a cmdlet were run with a specific set of parameters.

Using External Commands

Because Windows PowerShell runs within the context of the Windows command prompt, you can run all Windows command-line commands, utilities, and graphical applications from within the Windows PowerShell, either at the PowerShell prompt or in your scripts. However, it is important to remember that the Windows PowerShell interpreter parses all commands before passing off the command to the command-prompt environment. If the Windows PowerShell has a like-named command, keyword, alias, or function for a command, this command, and not the expected Windows command, is executed. (See Chapter 4, "Initializing the Scripting

Environment" and Chapter 5, "Navigating Input, Parsing, and Output Options" later in this text for more information on aliases and functions.)

Non–Windows PowerShell commands and programs must reside in a directory that is part of the PATH environment variable. If the item is found in the path, it is run. The PATH variable also controls where the Windows PowerShell looks for applications, utilities, and scripts. In Windows PowerShell, you can work with Windows environment variables by using $env. If you want to view the current settings for the PATH environment variable, you type **$env:path**. If you want to add a directory to this variable, you can use the following syntax:

```
$env:path += ";DirectoryPathToAdd"
```

Here, *DirectoryPathToAdd* is the directory path you want to add to the path, such as:

```
$env:path += ";C:\Scripts"
```

> **NOTE**   In Windows PowerShell, the dollar sign ($) indicates a variable. Normally, when you work with user-created variables, you assign a specified value to a variable, such as the results of a query, and then work with the variable using its $-prefixed name. In this example, you are accessing the PATH environment variable through the Env provider and the required syntax to do this is as shown.

To have this directory added to the path every time you start Windows PowerShell, you can add the command as an entry in a PowerShell profile. A profile is a type of script used to set the working environment for PowerShell. Keep in mind that cmdlets are like built-in commands rather than stand-alone executables.

Because of this, they are not affected by the PATH environment variable.

> **REAL WORLD** Computers running Windows and Windows Server have the SETX utility. With the SETX utility, you can write environment variable changes directly to the Windows registry, which makes the changes permanent rather than temporary, as the $env:path command does. You can also use SETX to obtain current registry key values and write them to a text file.

Understanding Scripts & Script Execution

Windows PowerShell scripts are text files with the .ps1 extension. You can enter any command or cmdlet that you can run at the PowerShell prompt into a script by copying the related command text to a file and saving the file with the .ps1 extension. You can then run the script in the same way you would any other command or cmdlet. However, when you are working with PowerShell scripts, the current directory might not be part of the environment path. For this reason, you might need to use "./" when you run a script in the current directory. For example, if you create a PowerShell script called run_all.ps1, and the script is in the current directory, you could run the script by entering the following command:

```
./run_all
```

> **NOTE** PowerShell is designed to accommodate users with backgrounds in UNIX or Windows operating systems. You can use a forward slash or backward slash as a directory separator. Following this, you can enter **./run_all** or **.\run_all** to reference a script in the current working directory.

Whenever you work with scripts, you need to keep in mind the current execution policy and whether signed scripts are required.

The current execution policy for Windows PowerShell controls whether and how you can run configuration files and scripts. Execution policy is a built-in security feature of Windows PowerShell that is set on a per-user basis in the Windows registry. Although the default configuration depends on which operating system and edition is installed, you can quickly determine the execution policy by entering **get-executionpolicy** at the PowerShell prompt.

The available execution policies, from most secure to least secure, are:

- **Restricted**   Does not load configuration files or scripts. This means all configuration files and scripts, regardless of whether they are signed or unsigned. Because a profile is a type of script, profiles are not loaded either.
- **AllSigned**   Requires all configuration files and scripts from all sources—whether local or remote—to be signed by a trusted publisher. Because of this requirement, configuration files and scripts on the local computer must be signed as configuration files, and scripts from remote computers must be signed. PowerShell prompts you before running scripts from trusted publishers.
- **RemoteSigned**   Requires all configuration files and scripts from remote sources to be signed by a trusted publisher. Configuration files and scripts on the local computer do not need to be signed. PowerShell does not prompt you before running scripts from trusted publishers.

- **Unrestricted** Allows all configuration files and scripts to run whether they are from local or remote sources and regardless of whether they are signed or unsigned. However, if you run a configuration file or script from a remote resource, you are prompted with a warning that the file comes from a remote resource before the configuration file is loaded or the script runs.

> **REAL WORLD** The default execution policy setting for Windows Server 2012 R2 is RemoteSigned. For earlier versions of Windows Server as well as Windows 7 and later, the default execution policy setting is Restricted.

As you can see, execution policy determines whether you can load configuration files and run scripts as well as whether scripts must be digitally signed before they will run. When an execution policy prevents loading a file or running a script, a warning is displayed explaining applicable restrictions.

You can use Set-ExecutionPolicy to change the preference for the execution policy. Changes to the policy are written to the registry. However, if the Turn On Script Execution setting in Group Policy is enabled for the computer or user, the user preference is written to the registry, but it is not effective, and Windows PowerShell displays a message explaining the conflict. You cannot use Set-ExecutionPolicy to override a group policy, even if the user preference is more restrictive than the policy setting.

To set the execution policy to require that all scripts have a trusted signature to execute, enter the following command:

```
set-executionpolicy allsigned
```

To set the execution policy so that scripts downloaded from the Web execute only if they are signed by a trusted source, enter:

```
set-executionpolicy remotesigned
```

To set the execution policy to run scripts regardless of whether they have a digital signature and work in an unrestricted environment, you can enter the following command:

```
set-executionpolicy unrestricted
```

The change occurs immediately and is applied to the local console or application session. Because the change is written to the registry, the new execution policy will be used whenever you work with PowerShell.

> **NOTE** Because only administrators are allowed to change the execution policy, you must run Windows PowerShell with the Run As Administrator option.

Specifying Authentication Credentials

When you are working with cmdlets and scripts in PowerShell that modify system information, you might need to specify a credential for authentication. Whether in a script or at the prompt, the easiest way to do this is to use Get-Credential to obtain a Credential object and save the result in a variable for later use. Consider the following example:

```
$cred = get-credential
```

When PowerShell reads this command, PowerShell prompts you for a user name and password and then stores the credentials provided in the $cred variable. It is important to point out that the credentials prompt is displayed simply because you typed **Get-Credential**.

You also can specify that you want the credentials for a specific user in a specific domain. In the following example, you request the credentials for the TestUser account in the DevD domain:

```
$cred = get-credential -credential devd\testuser
```

A Credential object has UserName and Password properties that you can work with. Although the user name is stored as a regular string, the password is stored as a secure, encrypted string. Knowing this, you can reference the user name and password stored in $cred as follows:

```
$user = $cred.username
$password = $cred.password
```

3. Using the Help Documentation

Earlier in the text in "Working with Cmdlets," I introduced Get-Help. With Windows PowerShell 3.0 and later, help files aren't included with the standard installation and Windows PowerShell displays automatically generated help information by default. If you want to work with the full help documentation, you must either access the help files online or download updated help files to your computer.

Accessing Help Files

When working locally and not in a remote session, you can view help files for cmdlets online in the TechNet Library by adding the –Online parameter whenever you use Get-Help, such as:

```
get-help new-variable -online
```

If a computer doesn't have an Internet connection or you are working in a remote session, you won't be able to get online help and instead will need to rely on the default help files or help files that have been downloaded and installed on the computer. To download and install the current version of help files, enter the following command at an elevated, administrator PowerShell prompt:

```
update-help
```

When you run Update-Help without specifying additional parameters, Windows PowerShell attempts to connect to the Internet and download the help files from Microsoft's website. These actions will only be successful when the computer has a connection to the Internet and the connection isn't blocked by firewall rules or Internet privacy settings.

> **REAL WORLD** Running Update-Help from an administrator prompt is recommended as a best practice, but it is not required. By default, Update-Help downloads and installs the newest help file for modules available on a computer as well as modules in a remote session. If help files were previously installed, Update-Help only updates the help files that have been modified since they were installed. However, if you run Update-Help with standard permissions, Update-Help will not download or install help files for modules in the PowerShell installation directory, including the Windows PowerShell Core modules. Thus, to ensure help files for all available modules are installed and updated, you must run Windows PowerShell with the Run As Administrator option.

Creating a Central Help Folder

Rather than downloading and installing help files on multiple computers or when computers don't have connections to the Internet, you may want to specify a central help location for your organization and then install help files from this location as required. Installing and using help files from a central location is a two-step process:

1. You use Save-Help to download help files and save them to a specified folder or network share.

2. You use Update-Help to install help files from the central location.

With you are working with Save-Help, you specify the destination path using the –DestinationPath parameter, such as:

```
Save-Help -DestinationPath C:\HelpFiles
```

Or

```
Save-Help -DestinationPath \\Server54\PS_Help
```

As long as the destination paths exist and you have permission to write to the location, you'll be able to save the help files. In these instances, here's how Save-Help works with PowerShell 4.0 and later:

1. The PowerShell modules on the computer to which you are currently logged on as well as the modules in the current remote session determine which help files are used. When you run Save-Help, Save-Help identifies all the PowerShell modules installed on the current computer and in the current session.

2. Next, if the destination folder was previously used to save help files, Save-Help checks the version of the help files in the destination folder. If newer help files are available for the applicable PowerShell modules, Save-Help downloads the new help files and saves them in the destination folder.

> **REAL WORLD**   When you are working in a remote session, there's an important difference between the way Save-Help works with various versions of PowerShell. With PowerShell 3.0, the HelpInfoUri property, which identifies the location of help files online by their URL, is not preserved when remoting. Thus, Save-Help works only for modules installed on the local computer and does not apply to modules in the remote session. On the other hand, with PowerShell 4.0 or 5.0, the HelpInfoUri property is preserved when remoting. Thus, Save-Help is able to pass back the location of help files for modules that are installed on the remote computer,

> which in turn allows you to save help files for the modules installed on the remote computer.

Often, you'll need to pass in credentials to update help files. Use the –Credential parameter to do this. In the following example, you specify that the WilliamS account in the ImaginedL domain should be used to perform the update task:

```
Save-Help –DestinationPath \\Server54\PS_Help
-Credential ImaginedL\Williams
```

When you run the command, you are prompted for the password for the WilliamS account. The account's credentials are then used to write to the destination path.

Once you save help files to a central location, you can write the help files to any computer in your organization and in this way make the help files available locally. To do this, run Update-Help and use the –SourcePath parameter to specify the source location for the help files, such as:

```
Update-Help –SourcePath \\Server54\PS_Help
-Credential ImaginedL\Williams
```

Help files are language specific. Update-Help and Save-Help create language-specific files for all languages and locales configured on your management computer. Thus, if the Region And Language settings for your management computer specify the current locale as US English, the help commands create and work with the US English help files by default.

When you are working in an enterprise where computers are deployed using different languages, locales or both, it is important to note that a problem can occur when help files are saved with language or culture settings that are different from the language and culture settings of your management computer. For example, if help files were saved with the current locale set as US English but you are working with a computer with the current locale set as UK English, you won't be able to retrieve the help files for that locale from the source location. An easy work around is to save help files to the central share using computers that have the appropriate languages and cultures configured.

4. Initializing the Scripting Environment

Windows PowerShell provides a dynamic, extensible execution environment. You can initialize the environment for PowerShell in several ways, including passing startup parameters to Powershell.exe, using a customized profile, using a console file, or any combination of the three. You can extend the environment for PowerShell in several ways as well, including by installing providers and registering snap-ins.

Passing Startup Parameters

When you start PowerShell with standard user privileges rather than administrator privileges, you won't be able to perform many administrative tasks. To start PowerShell with administrator privileges, you must run the PowerShell console in elevated, administrator mode as discussed earlier.

When you run PowerShell from the Start screen or the Start menu, you can't pass in arguments. However, when you start PowerShell using the Search box, the Run dialog box or by entering **powershell** in an open command-shell window, you can pass arguments to PowerShell, including switches that control how PowerShell works and parameters that execute additional commands. For example, you can start PowerShell in no-logo mode (meaning the logo banner is turned off) by using the startup command **powershell -nologo**. By default, when you start PowerShell via the command shell and run a command, PowerShell initializes, runs the command and then exits. If you want PowerShell to execute a command and not terminate, type **powershell /noexit** followed by the command.

Listing 1 shows the basic syntax for invoking the PowerShell console. Table 4 lists the available startup parameters. By default, startup profiles are loaded when the PowerShell console starts. You can exit the console at any time by typing **exit** and then pressing Enter.

LISTING 1 PowerShell Syntax

```
powershell[.exe] [-PSConsoleFile FileName | -Version
VersionNum] -NoLogo] [-NoExit] [-NoProfile]
[-NonInteractive] [-Sta] [-InputFormat {Text | XML}]
[-OutputFormat {Text | XML}] [-WindowsStyle Style]
[-EncodedCommand Base64EncodedCommand] [-File
ScriptFilePath] [-ExecutionPolicy PolicySetting]
[-Command CommandText]
```

TABLE 4 PowerShell Startup Parameters

PARAMETER	DESCRIPTION
–Command	Specifies the command text to execute as though it were typed at the PowerShell command prompt.
–EncodedCommand	Specifies the base64-encoded command text to execute.
–ExecutionPolicy	Sets the default execution policy for the console session.
–File	Sets the name of a script file to execute.
–InputFormat	Sets the format for data sent to PowerShell as either text string or serialized XML. The default format is XML. Valid values are *text* and *XML*.
-Mta	Starts PowerShell is multi-threaded mode.

PARAMETER	DESCRIPTION
−NoExit	Does not exit after running startup commands. This parameter is useful when you run PowerShell commands or scripts via the command prompt (cmd.exe).
−NoLogo	Starts the PowerShell console without displaying the copyright banner.
−Noninteractive	Starts the PowerShell console in noninteractive mode. In this mode, PowerShell does not present an interactive prompt to the user.
−NoProfile	Tells the PowerShell console not to load the current user's profile.
−OutputFormat	Sets the format for output as either text string or serialized XML. The default format is text. Valid values are *text* and *XML*.
−PSConsoleFile	Loads the specified Windows PowerShell console file. Console files end with the .psc1 extension and can be used to ensure that specific snap-in extensions are loaded and available. You can create a console file using Export-Console in Windows PowerShell.
−Sta	Starts PowerShell in single-threaded mode. This is the default.
−Version	Sets the version of Windows PowerShell to use for compatibility, such as 1.0.

PARAMETER	DESCRIPTION
–WindowStyle	Sets the window style as Normal, Minimized, Maximized, or Hidden. The default is Normal.

> **TIP**   If you want PowerShell to always start with specific parameters, you can modify the shortcut used to start PowerShell. For example, if the taskbar has a shortcut for Windows PowerShell, you can right-click this shortcut and select Properties to display the Properties dialog box for the shortcut. On the Shortcut tab, you would then edit the Target property by adding the parameters and any related parameter values required to the existing value and then clicking OK to save the changes. For example, after the full path to powershell.exe, you could add –NoLogo to always start PowerShell without displaying the standard banner.

Invoking Windows PowerShell

Although you'll most often work with the PowerShell console or the PowerShell application, at times you might want to invoke PowerShell to run a cmdlet from the Windows command shell (cmd.exe) environment or a batch script. To do so, you use the –Command parameter. Generally, you will also want to suppress the Windows PowerShell logo with the –NoLogo parameter and stop execution of profiles with the –NoProfile parameter. For example, at a command prompt or in a batch script, you could get a list of running processes via PowerShell with the following command:

```
powershell -nologo -noprofile -command get-process
```

When you enter this command, the Windows command shell runs PowerShell as it would any other external program, passing in the parameters and parameter values you use and then exiting PowerShell when execution completes. If you want the command shell to run a PowerShell command and remain in PowerShell after execution, you can add the –NoExit parameter as shown in the following example:

```
powershell -noexit -command get-process
```

Using –Command to Run Commands

Because –Command is the most common parameter you'll use when invoking PowerShell from a command prompt or batch script, let's take a closer look at all the ways it can be used. If you enter – as the command, the command text is read from standard input. You also can use piping and redirection techniques to manipulate the output of a command. However, keep in mind that any characters typed after the command are interpreted as command arguments. Because of this, to write a command that includes piping or redirection, you must enclose the command text in double quotation marks. The following example gets information about currently running processes and sorts it by process identifier:

```
powershell -nologo -noprofile -command "get-process |
sort-object Id"
```

> **REAL WORLD** Most commands generate output that can be redirected to another command as input. To do this, you use a technique called *piping*, whereby the output of a command is sent as the input of the next command. Following this, you can see the general syntax for piping is:

> Command1 | Command2
>
> where the pipe redirects the output of Command1 to the input of Command2. But you can also redirect output more than once by using this syntax:
>
> Command1 | Command2 | Command3
>
> Generally, if a cmdlet accepts input from another cmdlet, the cmdlet will have an –InputObject parameter and you can pipe output to the cmdlet.

Windows PowerShell also supports script blocks. A script block is a series of commands executed in sequence. Script blocks are enclosed in braces ({}), and each command within a script block is separated by a semicolon. Although you can enter script blocks enclosed in braces, you can do so directly only when running Powershell.exe in Windows PowerShell. The results are then returned as deserialized XML objects rather than standard objects. For example, if you are already working at the PowerShell prompt and want to run a series of commands through an isolated PowerShell instance, you can do so by enclosing the commands in braces and separating commands with semicolons, as shown in this example:

```
powershell -command {get-service; get-process}
```

Although this technique works if you are already working with the PowerShell prompt, it doesn't work when you want to run PowerShell from a command prompt. The workaround is to use the following format:

```
"& {CommandText}"
```

Here, the quotation marks indicate a string, and the ampersand (&) is an invoke operator that causes the command to be executed. After you write a string that runs a command, you will generally be able to run the command at either the command prompt or the PowerShell prompt. For example, even though you cannot enter powershell -command {get-service; get-process} at the command prompt, you can enter the following at a command prompt:

```
powershell -command "& {get-service; get-process}"
```

Here, you pass a code block to PowerShell as a string to parse and execute. PowerShell executes Get-Service and displays the results and then executes Get-Process and displays the results. If you want one syntax that will generally succeed whether you are working with strings, multiple commands, the command prompt, or the PowerShell prompt, this syntax is the one you should use.

Using –File to Run Scripts

When you are working with the Windows command shell and want to run a PowerShell script, you also can use piping and redirection techniques to manipulate the output of a command. However, instead of using the –Command parameter, you use the –File parameter to specify the script to run. As shown in the following example, you follow the –File parameter with the path to the script to run:

```
powershell -nologo -noprofile -file
c:\scripts\run_all.ps1
```

If the script is in the current directory, simply enter the script name:

```
powershell -nologo -noprofile -file run_all.ps1
```

If the path name includes blank spaces, you must enclose the path in double quotation marks, as shown in this example:

```
powershell -nologo -noprofile -file "c:\data\current
scripts\run_all.ps1"
```

> **REAL WORLD** You can specify parameters whether you start PowerShell from a taskbar shortcut or a command prompt. When starting PowerShell from the taskbar, edit the shortcut to specify parameters you want to use whenever you work with PowerShell. To do so, follow these steps:

1. On the taskbar, right-click the shortcut and then select Properties.

2. In the Properties dialog box, the Target entry on the Shortcut tab is selected by default.

3. Without pressing any other key, press the Right arrow key. This places the insertion cursor at the end of the full path to PowerShell. Insert a space, and then type your parameters and parameter values.

4. Click OK to save the settings. If you make a mistake or no longer want to use parameters, repeat this procedure and remove any parameters and values you've added.

Using Nested Consoles

Sometimes you might want to use different environment settings or parameters for a PowerShell console and then go back to your original settings without exiting the console window. To do this, you can use a technique called *nesting*. With nesting, you start a PowerShell console within another PowerShell console.

Unlike the command shell, the nested console opens with a new working environment and does not inherit its environment settings from the current console. You can work in this separate console environment and execute commands and scripts. When you type **exit** to close the instance of the nested console, you return to the previous console, and the previous environment settings are restored.

5. Navigating Input, Parsing, and Output Options

As you've seen from examples in this text, typing commands at the PowerShell prompt is a fairly straightforward process. The most basic approach is simply to type your command text and then press Enter. When you press Enter, PowerShell processes and parses the command text.

Using Basic Line Editing Techniques

The PowerShell console includes some basic editing capabilities for the current line. Table 5 lists the editing keys. Alternatively, enter **get-history** to list all the commands in the command history, or enter **clear-history** to clear the command history. Get-History lists commands by command number, and you can pass this to Invoke-History to run a specific numbered command from your command history. In this example, you run command 35:

```
invoke-history 35
```

TABLE 5 Basic Editing Keys

KEY	USAGE
`	Press the backward apostrophe key to insert a line break or as an escape character to make a literal character. You can also break a line at the pipe (|) character.
Alt+Space+E	Displays an editing shortcut menu with Mark, Copy, Paste, Select All, Scroll, and Find options. You can then press K for Mark, Y for Copy, P for Paste, S for Select All, L to scroll through the screen buffer, or F to search for text in the screen buffer. To copy the screen buffer to the Clipboard, press Alt+Space+E+S and then press Alt+Space+E+Y.
Alt+F7	Clears the command history.
Ctrl+C	Press Ctrl+C to break out of the subprompt or terminate execution.
Ctrl+End	Press Ctrl+End to delete all the characters in the line after the cursor.
Ctrl+Left arrow / Ctrl+Right arrow	Press Ctrl+Left arrow or Ctrl+Right arrow to move left or right one word at a time.
Ctrl+S	Press Ctrl+S to pause or resume the display of output.
Delete / Backspace	Press Delete to delete the character under the cursor, or press the Backspace key to delete the character to the left of the cursor.

KEY	USAGE
Esc	Press the Esc key to clear the current line.
F1	Moves the cursor one character to the right on the command line. At the end of the line, inserts one character from the text of your last command.
F2	Creates a new command line by copying your last command line up to the character you type.
F3	Completes the command line with the content from your last command line, starting from the current cursor position to the end of the line.
F4	Deletes characters from your current command line, starting from the current cursor position up to the character you type.
F5	Scans backward through your command history.
F7	Displays a pop-up window with your command history and allows you to select a command. Use the arrow keys to scroll through the list. Press Enter to select a command to run, or press the Right arrow key to place the text on the command line.
F8	Uses text you've entered to scan backward through your command history for commands that match the text you've typed so far on the command line.
F9	Runs a specific numbered command from your command history. Command numbers are listed when you press F7.

KEY	USAGE
Home / End	Press Home or End to move to the beginning or end of the line.
Insert	Press Insert to switch between insert mode and overwrite mode.
Left / Right arrow keys	Press the Left or Right arrow key to move the cursor left or right on the current line.
Page Up / Page Down	Press the Page Up or Page Down key to access the first or last command in the command history.
Right-click	If QuickEdit is disabled, displays an editing shortcut menu with Mark, Copy, Paste, Select All, Scroll, and Find options. To copy the screen buffer to the Clipboard, right-click, choose Select, and then press Enter.
Tab / Shift+Tab	Press the Tab key or press Shift+Tab to access the tab expansion function.
Up / Down arrow keys	Press the Up or Down arrow key to scan forward or backward through your command history, as discussed in "Using the Command History" in Chapter 1 earlier in this text.
Windows key+R and then type **powershell**	Runs Windows PowerShell. However, if you've installed multiple versions of PowerShell or are using a 64-bit computer, the first version encountered runs (and this is not necessarily the one you want to use).

REAL WORLD   The way copying and pasting text works in the PowerShell console depends on whether QuickEdit mode is enabled or disabled. With QuickEdit enabled, you copy text by dragging the mouse and pressing Enter, and then paste text by clicking the mouse. When you drag the mouse to select text to copy, be careful not to pause momentarily when you start; otherwise, PowerShell will paste from the Clipboard. With QuickEdit disabled, you copy by right-clicking, selecting Mark, dragging the mouse to select the text, and then pressing Enter. You paste by right-clicking and selecting Paste. You can enable or disable QuickEdit using the Properties dialog box, as described in the "Managing Windows PowerShell Console Properties" earlier in this text.

How Parsing Works

In addition to the processing modes discussed previously in "Passing Startup Parameters," PowerShell also has parsing modes. Don't confuse processing modes with parsing modes. Processing modes control the way PowerShell processes commands. Generally speaking, processing occurs either interactively or noninteractively. Parsing modes control the way PowerShell parses each value within a command line.

PowerShell breaks down command lines into units of execution and tokens. A unit of execution includes everything from the first character on a line to either a semicolon or the end of a line. A token is a value within a unit of execution. Knowing this, you can:

▪ Enter multiple commands on a single command line by using semicolons to separate each command.
▪ Mark the end of a unit of execution by pressing Enter.

The way PowerShell parses values is determined by the first token encountered when parsing a unit of execution. PowerShell parses using one of these modes:

- **Expression mode** PowerShell uses expression mode when the first token encountered in a unit of execution *is not* the name of a cmdlet, keyword, alias, function, or external utility. PowerShell evaluates expressions as either numerical values or strings. Character string values must be contained in quotation marks, and numbers not in quotation marks are treated as numerical values (rather than as a series of characters).
- **Command mode** PowerShell uses command mode when the first token encountered in a unit of execution is the name of a cmdlet, keyword, alias, function, or external utility. PowerShell invokes command tokens. Values after the command token are handled as expandable strings except when they start with a special character that denotes the start of a variable, array, string, or subexpression. These special characters include $, @, ', " and (, and when these characters are encountered, the value is handled using expression mode.

With these rules in mind, you can see that the following are true:

- If you enter 5+5 at the PowerShell prompt, PowerShell interprets 5+5 as an expression to evaluate and displays the result as 10.
- If you enter Write-Host 5+5 at the PowerShell prompt, PowerShell interprets 5+5 as an argument to Write-Host and displays 5+5.

▪ If you enter Write-Host (5+5) at the PowerShell prompt, PowerShell interprets (5+5) as an expression to evaluate and then pass to Write-Host. As a result, PowerShell displays 10.

Parsing Assigned Values

In PowerShell, variable definitions begin with the dollar sign ($) and are followed by the name of the variable you are defining. To assign a value to a variable, you use the equals sign (=) and then specify the value you want. After you create a variable, you can reference or display the value of the variable by using the variable name.

Following this, if you enter $a = 5+5 at the PowerShell prompt, PowerShell interprets 5+5 as an expression to evaluate and assigns the result to the variable a. As a result, when you write the value of $a to the PowerShell prompt by entering

```
$a
```

or by entering

```
Write-Host $a
```

the output is

```
10
```

On the other hand, let's say you define a variable named $a and assign it a string value, such as:

```
$a = "This is a string."
```

Here, the value assigned to $a is handled as a literal string, and the string is processed in expression mode. You know this because when you write the value of $a to the PowerShell prompt by entering

```
$a
```

or by entering

```
Write-Host $a
```

the output is

```
This is a string.
```

Sometimes, however, you'll want to force PowerShell to interpret a string literal expression using command mode. To see why, consider the following example:

```
$a = "Get-Process"
```

If you write the value of $a to the PowerShell prompt by entering

```
$a
```

the output is

```
Get-Process
```

This occurs because the value assigned to $a is handled as a literal string, and the string is processed in expression mode. However, you might have wanted PowerShell to actually run the Get-Process cmdlet. To do this, you need PowerShell to parse the string and determine that it contains a token that should be processed in command mode. You can accomplish this by using the & operator when you reference the $a variable, as shown in this example:

```
&$a
```

Because PowerShell processes the string in command mode, Get-Process is seen as a command token, the Get-Process cmdlet is invoked, and the output displays the currently running processes. This technique can be used with any cmdlet, keyword, alias, function, or external utility name assigned to a variable in a string. However, if you want to add values in addition to the command name, for example parameters, or use multiple commands or piping, you must enclose your command or commands in curly braces rather than quotation marks. This denotes a script block. Here is an example:

```
$a = {get-eventlog -newest 25 -logname application}
```

The value assigned to $a is handled as a special string, and the string is processed in expression mode. You know this because when you write the value of $a to the PowerShell prompt, the output is:

```
get-eventlog -newest 25 -logname system
```

You can force PowerShell to parse the contents of the script block by using:

```
&$a
```

PowerShell will then parse each token in the script block. The result will be the same as when you enter the command text.

Parsing Exceptions

When you enter part of an expression on the command line but do not complete the expression, PowerShell displays the > >

subprompt, indicating that it is waiting for you to complete the expression. For example, if you type **Write-Host (** and press Enter, PowerShell displays the >> subprompt and waits for you to complete the expression. You must then complete the command line by entering any additional required text, such as **5+5)**, and then press Enter. You must then press Enter again (without typing any additional text) to exit the subprompt and return. PowerShell then interprets this input as a completed unit of execution.

If you want to intentionally split command text across multiple lines of input, you can use the backward apostrophe character (`). This technique is handy when you are copying long command lines and pasting them into a PowerShell console so that you can run them. Here's how this works:

1. Enter part of the command text, and then type `. When you press Enter, PowerShell displays the >> subprompt.

2. Enter the next part of the command text. Then either enter ` to indicate that you want to continue the command text on the next line or press Enter to mark the end of the command text.

3. When you finally mark the end of the line by pressing Enter without using the backward apostrophe (and you've closed all expressions), PowerShell parses the command text as appropriate.

An example and partial output follows:

```
get-eventlog -newest 25 `
>> -logname system
>>
```

```
Index Time     EntryType    Source           InstanceID Message
----- ----     ---------    ------           ---------- -------
258248 Feb 28 16:12    Information Service Control M...
1073748860 The description for Event ID '1073748860' in
So...
258247 Feb 28 14:27    Information Service Control M...
1073748860 The description for Event ID '1073748860' in
So...
```

If your command text uses the pipe (|) character, you can also
break a line and continue it on the next line at the pipe
character, as shown in the following example and partial output:

```
get-process |
>>   sort-object Id
>>
```

Handles	NPM(K)	PM(K)	WS(K)	VM(M)	CPU(s)	Id	ProcessName
0	0	0	24	0		0	Idle
710	0	0	12904	20		4	System
28	1	360	816	4		516	smss
666	6	1872	5212	94		592	csrss

Output from Parsing

After parsing commands and values, PowerShell returns output.
Unlike with the command shell (Cmd.exe), built-in commands
that you run in PowerShell return objects in the output. An
object is a collection of data points that represent an item.
Objects have a specific data type, such as String, Boolean, or
Numeric, and have methods and properties. Object methods
allow you to perform actions on the item the object represents.
Object properties store information about the item the object
represents. When you work with PowerShell, you can use an
object's methods and properties to take specific actions and
manipulate data.

When you combine commands in a pipeline, the commands pass information to each other as objects. When the first command runs, it sends one or more objects along the pipeline to the second command. The second command receives the objects from the first command, processes the objects, and then displays output or passes new or modified objects to the next command in the pipeline. This continues until all commands in the pipeline run and the final command's output is displayed. Because you and I can't read objects, PowerShell translates the objects for output on the screen as text. You can manipulate this output in many ways.

6. Managing Output

Although PowerShell reads and writes objects, the various values associated with objects are converted to text as a final part of the cmdlet execution process. When output is written to the console, this output is said to be written to the *standard output stream*. PowerShell supports other output streams as well. Before I describe these output streams, however, I'll explain how output is formatted by default.

Using Formatting Cmdlets

When you are working with external utilities and programs, those utilities and programs determine how the output is formatted. With PowerShell cmdlets, PowerShell calls designated formatting cmdlets to format the output for you. The formatter determines which properties of the output are displayed and whether they are displayed in a list or table. The formatter makes this determination based on the type of data being displayed. Strings and objects are handled and processed in different ways.

> **NOTE** The formatting cmdlets arrange the data to be displayed but do not actually display it. The output cmdlets, discussed next, are responsible for displaying output.

Specifying Output Format

You can explicitly specify the output format by using one of the following formatting cmdlets:

- **Format-List** Formats the output as a list of properties. All properties of the objects are formatted by default, with each property displayed on a separate line. Use –Properties to specify which properties to display by name. Enter property names in a comma-separated list. Use wildcard characters such as * to match any value as necessary.

```
Format-List [[-Property] PropertyName] [-DisplayError]
[-Expand String] [-Force] [-GroupBy Object]
[-InputObject Object] [-ShowError] [-View String]
```

- **Format-Table** Formats the output as a table with selected properties of the objects in each column. The object type determines the default layout and the properties that are displayed. Use –AutoSize to automatically adjust the column size and number of columns based on the width of the data. Use –HideTableHeaders to omit column headings. Use –Wrap to display text that exceeds the column width on the next line.

```
Format-Table [[-Property] PropertyName] [-AutoSize]
[-DisplayError] [-Expand String] [-Force] [-GroupBy
Object] [-HideTableHeaders] [-InputObject Object]
[-ShowError] [-View String] [-Wrap]
```

- **Format-Wide** Formats the output as a multicolumned table, but only one property of each object is displayed. Use –AutoSize to automatically adjust the column size and number of columns based on the width of the data. Use –Columns to specify the number of columns to display.

```
Format-Wide [[-Property] PropertyName] [-AutoSize]
[-Column NumColumns] [-DisplayError]
[-Expand String] [-Force] [-GroupBy Object]
[-InputObject Object] [-ShowError] [-View String]
```

- **Format-Custom** Formats the output using a predefined alternate view. You can determine the alternate view by reviewing the *format.PS1XML files in the Windows PowerShell directory. To create your own views in new .PS1XML files, use the Update-FormatData cmdlet to add them to Windows PowerShell. Use –Depth to specify the number of columns to display.

```
Format-Custom [[-Property] PropertyName] [-Depth Num]
[-DisplayError] [-Expand String] [-Force] [-GroupBy
Object] [-InputObject Object] [-ShowError] [-View String]
```

When working with the previous formatting cmdlets, you might also want to use these cmdlets:

• **Group-Object**   Groups objects that contain the same value for specified properties. Objects are grouped in sequence, so if values aren't sorted you won't get the result you want. Use –CaseSensitive to use case-sensitive grouping rather than the default grouping, which is not case sensitive. Use –NoElement to omit the names of members of the group, such as file names if you are grouping files by extension.

```
Group-Object [[-Property] PropertyName] [-AsHashTable]
[-AsString] [-CaseSensitive] [-Culture String]
[-InputObject Object] [-NoElement]
```

• **Sort-Object**   Sorts objects in ascending order based on the values of properties of the object. Use –Descending to reverse sort. Use –CaseSensitive to use case-sensitive sorting rather than the default sorting, which is not case sensitive. Use –Unique to eliminate duplicates and return only the unique members of a specified collection.

```
Sort-Object [[-Property] PropertyName] [-CaseSensitive]
[-Culture String] [-Descending] [-InputObject Object]
[-Unique]
```

To change the format of the output from any cmdlet, use the pipeline operator (|) to send the output of the command to a formatter. For example, the default format for the Get-Service cmdlet is a table that displays the value of the Status, Name, and DisplayName properties, as shown in this command and sample output:

```
get-service
```

```
Status    Name           DisplayName
------    ----           -----------
Stopped   ADWS           Active Directory Web Services
Stopped   AeLookupSvc    Application Experience
Stopped   ALG            Application Layer Gateway Service
Running   AppHostSvc     Application Host Helper Service
Stopped   AppIDSvc       Application Identity
Running   Appinfo        Application Information
Stopped   AppMgmt        Application Management
Stopped   AppReadiness   App Readiness
Stopped   AppXSvc        AppX Deployment Service (AppXSVC)
```

Format-Wide formats the output as a multicolumned table, but only one property of each object is displayed. The following command sends the output of a Get-Service cmdlet to the Format-Wide cmdlet:

```
get-service | format-wide -column 3
```

```
ADWS           AeLookupSvc          ALG
AppHostSvc     AppIDSvc             Appinfo
AppMgmt        AppReadiness         AppXSvc
aspnet_state   AudioEndpointBuilder Audiosrv
```

As a result, the service data is formatted into multiple columns for each service. The output provides the name of each configured service.

Knowing the name of a service, you can then examine services by listing the value of each configured property. For example, the following command gets detailed information on the WinRM service:

```
get-service winrm | format-list

Name                : WinRM
DisplayName         : Windows Remote Management (WS-
Management)
Status              : Stopped
DependentServices   : {}
ServicesDependedOn  : {RPCSS, HTTP}
CanPauseAndContinue : False
CanShutdown         : False
CanStop             : False
ServiceType         : Win32ShareProcess
```

In this format, the data appears in a list instead of a table, and there is additional information about the service that the previous output formatting omitted.

Specifying Properties to Display

With any of the formatting cmdlets, you can use the –Properties parameter to specify properties to display by name. You can use wildcards such as * to match any value as necessary. For example, to display all the properties of the winlogon process, enter:

```
get-process winlogon | format-list -property *

__NounName          : Process
Name                : winlogon
Handles             : 168
VM                  : 56729600
WS                  : 6262784
```

```
PM                    : 1384448
NPM                   : 8288
Path                  : C:\Windows\system32\winlogon.exe
Company               : Microsoft Corporation
CPU                   : 0.40625
FileVersion           : 6.3.9600.16384
ProductVersion        : 6.3.9600.16384
Description           : Windows Logon Application
Product             : Microsoft Windows Operating System
Id                    : 496
PriorityClass         : High
HandleCount           : 168
WorkingSet            : 6262784
PagedMemorySize       : 1384448
PrivateMemorySize     : 1384448
VirtualMemorySize     : 56729600
```

To see all the properties of an object, send the output of a command to the Get-Member cmdlet. For example, to see all the properties of a service object, type:

```
get-service | get-member -membertype *property
```

```
   TypeName: System.ServiceProcess.ServiceController

Name                    MemberType      Definition
----                    ----------      ----------
Name                    AliasProperty   Name = ServiceName
RequiredServices        AliasProperty   RequiredServices
                                        = ServicesDependedOn
CanPauseAndContinue Property            bool
CanPauseAndContinue                     {get;}
CanShutdown             Property         bool CanShutdown {get;}
CanStop                 Property         bool CanStop {get;}
Container               Property
System.ComponentModel.IContainer Container {get;}
DependentServices     Property  System.ServiceProcess.
          ServiceController[] DependentServices {get;}
DisplayName     Property        string DisplayName {get;set;}
MachineName     Property        string MachineName {get;set;}
ServiceHandle           Property         System.Runtime.
```

```
         InteropServices.SafeHandle ServiceHandle {get;}
ServiceName     Property      string ServiceName {get;set;}
ServicesDependedOn  Property      System.ServiceProcess.
         ServiceController[] ServicesDependedOn {get;}
ServiceType         Property
System.ServiceProcess.ServiceType ServiceType {get;}
Site                Property
System.ComponentModel.ISite
                              Site {get;set;}
Status          Property
System.ServiceProcess.ServiceControllerStatus Status
{get;}
```

Because all these properties are in the object that Get-Service retrieves for each service, you can display any or all of them by using the –Property parameter. For example, the following command uses the Format-Table command to display only the Name, Status, ServiceType, and ServicesDependedOn properties of each service:

```
get-service | format-table Name, Status, ServiceType,
ServicesDependedOn


Name          Status   ServiceType ServicesDependedOn
----          ------   ----------- ------------------
ADWS          Stopped  Win32OwnProcess {}
AeLookupSvc   Stopped  Win32ShareProcess {}
ALG           Stopped  Win32OwnProcess {}
AppHostSvc    Running  Win32ShareProcess {}
AppIDSvc      Stopped  Win32ShareProcess {RpcSs, CryptSvc,
AppID}
Appinfo       Running  Win32ShareProcess {RpcSs, ProfSvc}
AppMgmt       Stopped  Win32ShareProcess {}
AppReadiness  Stopped  Win32ShareProcess {}
AppXSvc       Stopped  Win32ShareProcess {rpcss}
```

In addition to formatting output for display, you might want to group and sort objects. All the formatting cmdlets include the –GroupBy parameter, which allows you to group output based on a specified property.

Using the –GroupBy parameter produces the same results as sending the output to the Group-Object cmdlet and then sending the output to a formatting cmdlet. However, these techniques probably won't generate the output you are looking for because these approaches generate a new header each time a new value is encountered for the specified property. For example, with the Get-Service cmdlet, you can group services by status, such as Running or Stopped, by using the following command:

```
get-service | format-list –groupby status

      Status: Stopped
Name                    : WinRM
DisplayName             : Windows Remote Management (WS-
Management)
Status                  : Stopped
DependentServices       : {}
ServicesDependedOn      : {RPCSS, HTTP}
CanPauseAndContinue     : False
CanShutdown             : False
CanStop                 : False
ServiceType             : Win32ShareProcess


      Status: Running
Name                    : Wlansvc
DisplayName             : WLAN AutoConfig
Status                  : Running
DependentServices       : {}
```

```
ServicesDependedOn   : {Eaphost, RpcSs, Ndisuio,
nativewifip}
CanPauseAndContinue : False
CanShutdown          : True
CanStop              : True
ServiceType          : Win32ShareProcess
```

When you use Group-Object and group by status, you get a different result entirely:

```
get-service | group-object status

Count Name              Group
----- ----              -----
   68 Stopped
{System.ServiceProcess.ServiceControll
   89 Running
{System.ServiceProcess.ServiceControll
```

Although both outputs can be useful, neither produces the result you need if you want to see all stopped services and all started services in sequence. The workaround is to sort the objects first and then group them. You sort objects by using the Sort-Object cmdlet. Sort-Object supports sorting on a single property and sorting on multiple properties. You specify the property or properties to sort on with the –Property parameter and separate multiple properties with commas. For example, if you want to sort services by status and name, you can use the following command:

```
get-service | sort-object status, name | format-table -
groupby status

   Status: Stopped

Status    Name           DisplayName
------    ----           -----------
Stopped   ADWS           Active Directory Web Services
```

```
Stopped   AeLookupSvc        Application Experience
Stopped   ALG                Application Layer Gateway Service
Stopped   AppIDSvc           Application Identity
Stopped   AppMgmt            Application Management
Stopped   AppReadiness       App Readiness
Stopped   AppXSvc            AppX Deployment Service (AppXSVC)

     Status: Running

Status    Name               DisplayName
------    ----               -----------
Running   AppHostSvc         Application Host Helper Service
Running   Appinfo            Application Information
Running   BFE                Base Filtering Engine
Running   CertPropSvc        Certificate Propagation
Running   CryptSvc           Cryptographic Services
Running   DcomLaunch         DCOM Server Process Launcher
```

By default, properties are sorted in ascending order. You can
sort in descending order with the –Descending parameter. For
example, with the Get-Process cmdlet, sorting the working set in
descending order can help you identify processes that are using
the most resources on the computer. The command to do this
is:

```
get-process | sort-object ws –descending
```

Handles	NPM(K)	PM(K)	WS(K)	VM(M)	CPU(s)	Id	ProcessName
1434	93	268752	285920	681	51.39	1972	powershell
527	48	123184	142892	788	8.77	2648	ServerManager
980	103	113112	140340	1335	22.30	3020	mmc
1376	76	58204	111476	568	29.78	2844	explorer
371	25	89964	105580	580	1.97	3460	wsmprovhost
561	45	104328	102364	748	12.73	3540	ServerManager
1252	69	36092	88760	434	9.50	3344	explorer
528	69	62712	78176	796	8.52	940	mmc
532	22	64688	66092	602	0.77	1800	powershell
476	22	64488	64008	602	0.64	2576	powershell
199	20	13896	60528	148	0.69	1980	dwm

In the output, you'll likely see multiple occurrences of some processes, such as powershell or svchost. If you enter the following command:

```
get-process | sort-object name -unique
```

Handles	NPM(K)	PM(K)	WS(K)	VM(M)	CPU(s)	Id	ProcessName
199	20	13896	60528	148	0.69	1980	dwm
1376	76	58204	111476	568	29.78	2844	explorer
980	103	113112	140340	1335	22.30	3020	mmc
1434	93	268752	285920	681	51.39	1972	powershell
527	48	123184	142892	788	8.77	2648	ServerManager
652	27	37452	45184	157	2.63	1960	svchost
371	25	89964	105580	580	1.97	3460	wsmprovhost

In the output, you'll see only the first occurrence of each process. However, this doesn't give you a complete picture of how many processes are running and what resources are being used by those processes.

Writing to Output Streams

Windows PowerShell supports several Write cmdlets for writing to different output streams. The first thing to know about these cmdlets is that they don't actually render the output. They simply pipeline (send) the output to a specified output stream. Although some output streams modify formatting of the output, the job of actually rendering and finalizing output belongs to the Output cmdlets discussed in the next section.

The available output streams include the following:

- Standard output stream
- Verbose message stream

- Warning message stream
- Debugging message stream
- Error stream

Explicitly Writing Output

You can explicitly write output using one of the following output cmdlets:

- **Write-Host** Writes to the standard output stream and allows you to set the background color and foreground color for text. By default, any text you write is terminated with a newline character. Use –NoNewLine to write text without inserting a newline character. Use –Separator to specify a string to output between objects you are displaying. Use –Object to specify the object or string literal to display.

```
Write-Host [[-Object] Object] [-BackgroundColor Color]
[-ForegroundColor Color] [-NoNewline] [-Separator Object]
```

- **Write-Output** Sends a specified object down the pipeline to the next command or for display in the console. Because Write-Output accepts an input object, you can pipeline objects to it, and it in turn will pipeline objects to the next command or the console as appropriate.

```
Write-Output [[-InputObject] Object] [-NoEnumerate]
```

The main reason to use Write-Host is to take advantage of the formatting options it provides, which include alternative text and background colors. You use the –BackgroundColor parameter to set the background color for output text and the –ForegroundColor parameter to set the text color. The available colors are:

- Black, DarkBlue, DarkGreen, DarkCyan
- DarkRed, DarkMagenta, DarkYellow, Gray
- DarkGray, Blue, Green, Cyan
- Red, Magenta, Yellow, White

In the following example, you specify that you want black text on a yellow background:

```
write-host -backgroundcolor yellow -foregroundcolor black
"This is text!"

This is text!
```

> **NOTE** The Write-Host cmdlet writes output to the application that is hosting PowerShell. Typically, this is the PowerShell console (powershell.exe) or the PowerShell application (powershell_ise.exe). Other applications can host the PowerShell engine, and those applications may handle Write-Host output in a different way. This means that you'll want to use Write-Host only when you know which host application will be used and how the host application will handle Write-Host output.

The Write-Output cmdlet also writes to the standard output stream. Unlike Write-Host, which does not accept input objects, Write-Output accepts objects as input. However, the purpose of Write-Output is simply to send a specified object to the next command in the pipeline. If the command is the last in the pipeline, the object is displayed on the console.

One situation in which to use Write-Output is when you want to be explicit about what you are writing to output. For example:

```
get-process | write-output
```

Here, you pipeline the output of Get-Process to Write-Output to show you are writing output.

When you are using variables, Write-Output is also helpful for being explicit about output you are writing. Consider the following example:

```
$p = get-process; $p
```

Here you create the $p variable, store Process objects in it, and then write those objects to the output. To be explicit about the write operation, you can change the previous line of code to read as follows:

```
$p = get-process; write-output $p
```

Using Other Output Streams

When you want to work with output streams other than the standard output stream, use the following Write cmdlets:

- **Write-Debug** Writes debug messages to the console from a script or command. By default, debug messages are not displayed in the console and do not cause execution to halt. You can display debug messages using the –Debug parameter (which is common to all cmdlets) or the $DebugPreference variable. The –Debug parameter overrides the value of the $DebugPreference variable for the current command.

```
Write-Debug [-message] DebugMessage
```

- **Write-Error** Writes error messages to the console from a script or command. By default, error messages are displayed in the console but do not cause execution to halt. Using the –ErrorAction parameter (which is common to all cmdlets) or the $ErrorActionPreference variable, you can modify the behavior. The –ErrorAction parameter overrides the value of the $ErrorActionPreference variable for the current command.

```
Write-Error [-Message] String [-ErrorId String]
[-TargetObject Object] [AddtlParams]

Write-Error -ErrorRecord ErrorRecord [AddtlParams]

Write-Error -Exception Exception [-Category String]
[-TargetObject Object] [AddtlParams]

AddtlParams=
[-CategoryTargetName String] [-CategoryTargetType String]
[-CategoryReason String] [-CategoryActivity String]
[-RecommendedAction String]
```

- **Write-Warning**   Writes warning messages to the console from a script or command. By default, warning messages are displayed in the console but do not cause execution to halt. You can modify the behavior using either the –WarningAction parameter (which is common to all cmdlets) or the $WarningPreference variable. The –WarningAction parameter overrides the value of the $WarningPreference variable for the current command.

```
Write-Warning [-message] WarningMessage
```

- **Write-Verbose**   Writes verbose messages to the console from a script or command. By default, verbose messages are not displayed in the console and do not cause execution to halt. You can display verbose messages using the –Verbose parameter (which is common to all cmdlets) or the $VerbosePreference variable. The –Verbose parameter overrides the value of the $VerbosePreference variable for the current command.

```
Write-Verbose [-message] VerboseMessage
```

Write-Debug, Write-Error, Write-Warning, and Write-Verbose can each be managed using either a common parameter or a preference variable. In every case, the common parameters accept a value of $true or $false, and the preference variable accepts one of the following values:

- Stop
- Inquire
- Continue
- SilentlyContinue

For example, the $DebugPreference variable determines how PowerShell handles debugging messages. You can specify:

- $DebugPreference=Stop to display debug messages and stop executing.
- $DebugPreference=Inquire to display debug messages that ask whether you want to continue.
- $DebugPreference=Continue to display debug messages and continue with execution.
- $DebugPreference=SilentlyContinue to not display debug messages and continue execution without interruption.

The –Debug parameter overrides the value of the $DebugPreference variable for the current command. You can specify **–Debug $true** or **–Debug** to turn on debugging, or you can specify **–Debug $false** to suppress the display of debugging messages when the value of $DebugPreference is not SilentlyContinue.

> **MORE INFO** A parameter that accepts a $true or $false value is referred to as a switch parameter. Generally, with any switch parameter, you can simply specify the parameter name to indicate that you want to set the parameter to $true. However, if you don't want a parameter or option to be used, you must explicitly set the parameter or option to $false.

Rendering and Finalizing the Output

Whether you enter a single cmdlet, send output to other cmdlets using piping, or format output explicitly, the final part of parsing and displaying output is a hidden background call to an output cmdlet. By default, as the last part of the execution process, PowerShell calls the default output cmdlet, which is typically the Out-Host cmdlet.

You can explicitly specify the output cmdlet to use by sending the output to one of the following output cmdlets:

- **Out-File** Sends the output to a file. You must specify the path to the output file to use. If the output file exists, you can use the –Force parameter to overwrite it or the –Append parameter to add the output to the file. You can use Out-File instead of the standard redirection techniques discussed in the next section.

```
Out-File [-FilePath] String [[-Encoding] String]
[AddtlParams]

Out-File [[-Encoding] String] -LiteralPath String
[AddtlParams]

AddtlParams=
[-Append] [-Force] [-InputObject SObject] [-NoClobber]
[-Width NumChars]
```

- **Out-GridView**   Sends the output to a grid view window and displays the output in an interactive table. The grid view window supports sorting, grouping, copying, and filtering.

```
Out-GridView [-InputObject Object] [-Title WindowTitle]
[-Wait | -PassThru | -OutputMode Mode]
```

- **Out-Host**   Sends the output to the command line. Add the –Paging parameter to display one page of output at a time (similar to using the More command in the command shell).

```
Out-Host [-InputObject Object] [-Paging]
```

- **Out-Null**   Sends the output to the null port. This deletes the output without displaying it, which is useful for output that you don't need.

```
Out-Null [-InputObject Object]
```

- **Out-Printer**   Sends the output to the default printer or to a named printer. Use the –Name parameter to specify the UNC path to the printer to use, such as –Name "\\PrintServer85\LaserP45".

```
Out-Printer [[-Name] String] [-InputObject Object]
```

- **Out-String**   Converts the output of all objects to a single string and then sends the result to the console. Use the –Stream parameter to send the strings for each object separately. Use the –Width parameter to specify the number of characters to display in each line of output. Any additional characters are truncated. The default width is 80 characters.

```
Out-String [-InputObject Object] [-Width NumChars]
[-Stream]
```

All these cmdlets accept input objects, which means you can pipeline objects to them. The following example writes events from the application log to the C:\logs\app\current.txt file:

```
get-eventlog -newest 10 -logname application | out-file
-filepath c:\logs\app\current.txt
```

All these cmdlets also accept objects as input. The following example displays the currently running processes in a grid view window:

```
$p = get-process; $p | out-gridview
```

Figure 4 shows the command output in grid view. Here, you store the results of Get-Process in the $p variable. Next, you use a pipeline character to send the $p variable to Out-GridView.

You also could have achieved the same result by sending the output of Get-Process directly to Out-GridView, as shown in this example:

```
get-process | out-gridview
```

Handles	NPM(K)	PM(K)	WS(K)	VM(M)	CPU(s)	Id	ProcessName
30	3	1464	2204	12	0.00	1,088	cmd
109	10	2400	11684	96	12.05	2,412	conhost
61	7	1792	7868	54	0.02	3,372	conhost
57	6	1012	5236	51	0.08	3,816	conhost
60	7	1852	8592	56	0.34	3,852	conhost
247	11	1672	3572	44	0.77	376	csrss
269	21	1744	26328	64	18.13	436	csrss
179	15	1828	44652	86	1.14	2,468	csrss
242	20	3300	10780	58	0.55	1,200	dfsrs
103	8	1384	3748	22	0.02	1,788	dfssvc
253	33	26496	25260	573	0.11	1,448	dllhost
199	25	27500	60420	157	4.44	748	dwm
216	23	13988	64208	175	6.89	1,980	dwm
1,370	75	57816	111180	567	29.91	2,844	explorer
495	23	7132	24344	144	0.39	2,892	iexplore

Figure 4 Command output is displayed in the grid view.

More on Redirecting Input, Output, and Error

By default, commands take input from the parameters specified when they are called by PowerShell and then send their output, including errors, to the standard console window. Sometimes, however, you'll want to take input from another source or send output to a file or another output device, such as a printer. You might also want to redirect errors to a file rather than have them displayed in the console window. In addition to using the Output cmdlets discussed previously, you can perform these and other redirection tasks by using the techniques introduced in Table 6 and discussed in the examples that follow.

TABLE 6 Redirection Techniques for Input, Output, and Errors

REDIRECTION TECHNIQUE	DESCRIPTION
command1 | command2	Sends the output of the first command to be the input of the second command.
command > [path]filename	Sends output to the named file, creating the file if necessary or overwriting it if it already exists.
command >> [path]filename	Appends output to the named file if it exists or creates the file and then writes to it.
command 2> [path]filename	Creates the named file and sends any error output to it. If the file exists, it is overwritten.
command 2>> [path]filename	Appends errors to the named file if it exists or creates the file and then writes errors to it.
command 2>&1	Sends error output to the same destination as standard output.

Piping is the primary redirection technique, and you'll find examples of piping throughout this section. Another command redirection technique is to send output to a file. You can do this with the Out-File cmdlet. You also can use > to create or overwrite a named file, or >> to create or append data to a named file. For example, if you want to write the current status of running processes to a file, you can use the following command:

```
get-process > processes.txt
```

Unfortunately, if there is a file in the current directory with the same file name, this command overwrites the file and creates a new one. If you want to append this information to an existing file rather than overwrite an existing file, change the command text to read as follows:

```
get-process >> processes.txt
```

By default, errors from commands are written as output on the command line. As discussed previously, you can manage the error stream using Write-Error, the –ErrorAction parameter (which is common to all cmdlets), or the $ErrorActionPreference variable. Another way to redirect standard error is to tell PowerShell that errors should go to the same destination as standard output. To do this, type the 2>&1 redirection symbol as shown in this example:

```
chkdsk /r > diskerrors.txt 2>&1
```

Here, you send standard output and standard error to a file named Diskerrors.txt. If you want to track only errors, you can redirect only the standard error. In this example, standard output is displayed at the command line and standard error is sent to the file Diskerrors.txt:

```
chkdsk /r 2> diskerrors.txt
```

If the error file exists, it is overwritten automatically. To append to an existing file rather than overwrite it, you can use the append technique shown in the following example:

```
chkdsk /r 2>> diskerrors.txt
```

7. Working with Profiles

PowerShell scripts and profiles end with the .ps1 file extension. Generally speaking, profiles are always loaded when you work with Windows PowerShell, but there are specific exceptions. For example, when testing a script, you might want to invoke PowerShell without loading a profile and then run the script. Doing so will help ensure that you've coded the script properly and haven't used any profile-specific settings.

You use profiles to store frequently used elements, including:

- **Aliases**   An alias is an alternate name for a command, function, script, file, executable, or other command element. After you create an alias, you can use the alias as a keystroke shortcut or friendly name to invoke the related command element. For example, gsv is an alias for Get-Service. Instead of entering **get-service winrm** to get information about the WinRM service, you could enter **gsv winrm**. To list all available aliases, enter **get-alias** at the PowerShell prompt.

```
Get-Alias [[-Name] Strings] [-Exclude Strings]
[-Scope String]
```

```
Get-Alias [[-Definition] Strings] [-Exclude Strings]
[-Scope String]
```

- **Functions**   A function is a named set of PowerShell commands. When you call a function by its name, the set of commands runs just as though you had typed each command at the command line. For example, you could create a function to examine critical processes and services on a computer and generate a report. By adding the function to a profile, you would then be able to run the function at any time by entering the function name at the PowerShell prompt. To list all

available functions, enter **get-childitem function:** at the
PowerShell prompt.

```
Get-ChildItem [[-Path] Strings] [[-Filter] Strings]
[AddtlParams]

Get-ChildItem [[-Filter] String] -LiteralPath Strings
[AddtlParams]

Get-ChildItem [-Attributes FileAttributes] [-Directory]
[-File] [-Force] [-Hidden] [-ReadOnly] [-System]
[-UseTransaction [{$True|$False}]]

AddtlParams=
[-Exclude Strings] [-Force] [-Include Strings] [-Name]
[-Recurse] [-UseTransaction [{$True|$False}]]
```

- **Variables**   A variable is a placeholder for a value. In addition
to environment variables from the operating system,
PowerShell supports automatic, preference, and user-created
variables. To reference a variable at the prompt or in scripts,
you must precede the variable's name with a dollar sign ($).
For example, to reference the home variable, you must enter
$home. To list all available variables, enter **get-variable** at the
PowerShell prompt.

```
Get-Variable [[-Name] Strings] [-Exclude Strings]
[-Include Strings] [-Scope String] [-ValueOnly]
```

> **NOTE**   Your scripts and command text can use any of the
> available variables. Automatic variables are fixed and are
> used to store state information. Preference variables are
> changeable and are used to store working values for
> PowerShell configuration settings. By default, variables you
> create exist only in the current session and are lost when you
> exit or close the session. To maintain user-created variables,
> you must store them in a profile. For detailed information on
> variables.

> **TIP**   You can view the value of an automatic or a preference variable simply by entering its name at the PowerShell prompt. For example, to see the current value of the $home variable, enter **$home** at the PowerShell prompt. Environment variables are accessed in a slightly different way. You must reference $env: and then the name of the variable. For example, to display the value of the %ComputerName% variable, you must enter **$env:computername**.

Creating Profiles

You can create a profile by using a standard text editor. Simply enter the commands that define the aliases, functions, variables, or other elements you want to use, and then save the file with the appropriate file name in the appropriate location on your computer. That's it. This means you can use the following technique to create a profile:

1. In Notepad or any other text editor, enter the command text for the aliases, functions, variables, and any other command elements you want to use.

2. Save the file with the appropriate file name and file extension for a profile, such as Profile.ps1.

3. Copy the profile file to the appropriate location, such as a folder named $pshome.

When you are working with the PowerShell console and the PowerShell application, there are six types of profiles you need to know about. Table 7 summarizes these profiles. $home and $pshome are automatic variables. The $home variable stores the current user's home directory. The $pshome variable stores the installation directory for PowerShell.

TABLE 7 Common PowerShell Profiles

PROFILE TYPE	DESCRIPTION
Current User, PowerShell Console	A profile specific to the user account for the current user context and applicable only to the PowerShell console. Directory: $home\[My]Documents\WindowsPowerShell Name: profile.ps1
Current User, PowerShell ISE	A profile specific to the user account for the current user context and applicable only to the PowerShell application. Directory: $home\[My]Documents\WindowsPowerShell Name: Microsoft.PowerShellISE_profile.ps1
Current User, All Hosts	A profile specific to the current user context and applicable to both the PowerShell console and the PowerShell application. Directory: $home\[My]Documents Name: profile.ps1
All Users, PowerShell Console	A profile applicable to all users but specific to the PowerShell console. Directory: $pshome Name: Microsoft.PowerShell_profile.ps1
All Users, PowerShell ISE	A profile applicable to all users but specific to the PowerShell application. Directory: $pshome Name: Microsoft.PowerShellISE_profile.ps1
All Users, All Hosts	A profile applicable to all users for both the PowerShell console and the PowerShell application. Directory: $pshome Name: profile.ps1

When PowerShell starts, PowerShell looks for profiles in the specified locations and runs the profiles in the following order:

1. The All Users, All Hosts profile

2. Either the All Users, PowerShell or All Users, PowerShell ISE profile as appropriate

3. The Current User, All Hosts profile

4. Either the Current User, PowerShell or Current User, PowerShell ISE profile as appropriate

The order of the profiles' execution determines the precedence order for any conflicts. Whenever there is a conflict, the last value written wins. Following this, an alias defined in the Current User, PowerShell profile or the Current User, PowerShell ISE profile has precedence over any conflicting entries in any other profile.

> **TIP** As PowerShell downloads help files for a module no more than once per day, you can add Update-Help to your profile without worrying about PowerShell repeatedly downloading help files for a particular module. Note also that if your organization has a central save location for help files, updates are only available when new help files are downloaded and saved to that location.

Understanding Execution Order

Whenever you work with Windows PowerShell and PowerShell profiles, don't overlook the importance of execution order and the PATH environment variable. It is important to keep in mind where the commands you are using come from. PowerShell searches for commands in the following order:

1. **Aliases**   PowerShell looks for alternate built-in or profile-defined aliases for the associated command name. If an alias is found, the command to which the alias is mapped is run.

2. **Functions**   PowerShell looks for built-in or profile-defined functions with the command name. If a function is found, the function is executed.

3. **Cmdlets or language keywords**   PowerShell looks for built-in cmdlets or language keywords with the command name. If a cmdlet or language keyword is found, the appropriate action is taken.

4. **Scripts**   PowerShell looks for scripts with the .ps1 extension. If a PowerShell script is found, the script is executed.

5. **External commands and files**   PowerShell looks for external commands, non-PowerShell scripts, and utilities with the command name. If an external command or utility is found in a directory specified by the PATH environment variable, the appropriate action is taken. If you enter a file name, PowerShell uses file associations to determine whether a helper application is available to open the file.

Because of the execution order, contrary to what you might think, when you type **dir** and then press Enter to get a listing of the current directory, you are not running the dir command that is built into the Windows command shell (cmd.exe). Instead, when you type **dir** at the PowerShell prompt, you are actually running a PowerShell command. This command is called Get-ChildItem. Why does this occur? Although PowerShell does pass commands through to the Windows command shell, it does so only when a PowerShell command or an alias to a PowerShell command is not available. Because dir is a registered alias of Get-ChildItem, you are actually running Get-ChildItem when you enter **dir**.

Understanding the Command Path

The Windows operating system uses the command path to locate executables. The types of files that Windows considers to be executables are determined by the file extensions for executables. You can also map file extensions to specific applications by using file associations.

Managing the Command Path

You can view the current command path for executables by displaying the value of the PATH environment variable. To do this, open a PowerShell console, type **$env:path** on a line by itself, and then press Enter. The results should look similar to the following:

```
C:\Windows\System32;C:\Windows;C:\Windows\System32\Wbem;
C:\Windows\System32\WindowsPowerShell\v1.0\
```

> **NOTE** Observe the use of the semicolon (;) to separate individual paths. PowerShell uses the semicolon to determine where one file path ends and another begins.

The command path is set during logon using system and user environment variables, namely the %PATH% variable. The order in which directories are listed in the path indicates the search order PowerShell uses when it searches for executables. In the previous example, PowerShell searches in this order:

1. C:\Windows\System32
2. C:\Windows
3. C:\Windows\System32\Wbem
4. C:\Windows\System32\PowerShell\v1.0

You can permanently change the command path in the system environment by using the SETX command. For example, if you use specific directories for scripts or applications, you may want to update the path information. You can do this by using the SETX command to add a specific path to the existing path, such as **setx PATH "%PATH%;C:\Scripts"**.

> **NOTE** Observe the use of the quotation marks and the semicolon. The quotation marks are necessary to ensure that the value %PATH%;C:\Scripts is read as the second argument for the SETX command. As mentioned previously, the semicolon is used to specify where one file path ends and another begins. Because the command path is set when you open the PowerShell console, you must exit the console and open a new console to load the new path. If you'd rather not exit the console, you can update the PATH environment variable for the console as discussed in "Using External Commands" in Chapter 2 earlier in this text.

In this example, the directory C:\Scripts is appended to the existing command path, and the sample path listed previously would be modified to read as follows:

```
C:\Windows\System32;C:\Windows;C:\Windows\System32\Wbem;C
:\Windows\System32\PowerShell\v1.0;C:\Scripts
```

Don't forget about the search order that Windows uses. Because the paths are searched in order, the C:\Scripts directory will be the last one searched. This can sometimes slow execution of your scripts. To help Windows find your scripts faster, you may want C:\Scripts to be the first directory searched. In this case, you could set the command path by using the following command:

```
setx PATH "C:\Scripts;%PATH%"
```

Be careful when setting the command path. It is easy to overwrite all path information accidentally. For example, if you don't specify the %PATH% environment variable when setting the path, you will delete all other path information. One way to ensure that you can easily re-create the command path is to keep a copy of the command path in a file. To write the current command path to a file, type **$env:path > orig_path.txt**. Keep in mind that if you are using a standard console rather than an administrator console, you won't be able to write to secure system locations. In this case, you can write to a subdirectory to which you have access or your personal profile. To write the command path to the PowerShell console, type **$env:path**. Now you have a listing or a file that contains a listing of the original command path.

Managing File Extensions and File Associations

File extensions are what allow you to execute external commands by typing just their command name at the PowerShell prompt. Two types of file extensions are used:

- **File extensions for executables**   Executable files are defined with the %PATHEXT% environment variable. You can view the current settings by typing **$env:pathext** at the command line. The default setting is .COM;.EXE;.BAT;.CMD;.VBS;.VBE;.JS;.JSE;.WSF;.WSH;.MSC;.CPL. With this setting, the command line knows which files are executables and which files are not, so you don't have to specify the file extension at the command line.

- **File extensions for applications** File extensions for applications are referred to as *file associations*. File associations are what enable you to pass arguments to executables and to open documents, spreadsheets, or other application files by double-clicking file icons. Each known extension on a system has a file association that you can view by typing **cmd /c assoc** followed by the extension, such as **cmd /c assoc .exe**. Each file association in turn specifies the file type for the file extension. This information can be viewed using the FTYPE command followed by the file association, such as **cmd /c ftype exefile**.

NOTE Observe that you call ASSOC and FTYPE via the command shell. The reason is that they are internal commands for the command shell.

With executables, the order of file extensions sets the search order used by the command line on a per-directory basis. Thus, if a particular directory in the command path has multiple executables that match the command name provided, a .com file would be executed before a .exe file and so on.

Every known file extension on a system has a corresponding file association and file type—even extensions for executables. In most cases, the file type is the extension text without the period, followed by the keyword *file*, such as cmdfile, exefile, or batfile. The file association specifies that the first parameter passed is the command name and that other parameters should be passed on to the application.

You can look up the file type and file association for known extensions by using the ASSOC and FTYPE commands. To find the association, type **cmd /c assoc** followed by the file extension that includes the period. The output of the ASSOC

command is the file type. So if you type **cmd /c ftype**
association (where *association* is the output of the ASSOC
command), you'll see the file type mapping. For example, if you
type **cmd /c assoc .exe** to see the file associations for .exe
executables, you then type **cmd /c ftype exefile** to see the file
type mapping.

You'll see the file association is set to

```
exefile="%1" %*
```

Thus, when you run an .exe file, Windows knows the first value is
the command that you want to run and anything else you've
provided is a parameter to pass along.

TIP   File associations and types are maintained in the
Windows registry and can be set using the ASSOC and FTYPE
commands, respectively. To create the file association, type
cmd /c assoc followed by the extension setting, such as **cmd
/c assoc .pl=perlfile**. To create the file type, set the file type
mapping, including how to use parameters supplied with the
command name, such as cmd /c ftype
perlfile=C:\Perl\Bin\Perl.exe "%1" %*.

---

8. Executing Commands Remotely

Remote access in Windows PowerShell is made available through:

- PowerShell sessions which use the PowerShell remoting features.
- Common Information Model (CIM) sessions which use PowerShell remoting features by default (but also can use DCOM).
- PowerShell Web Access which allows you to connect to a web gateway application running on IIS, which in turns executes your remote commands.

NOTE   To work remotely, your computer and the remote computer must be properly configured. Individual cmdlets provide access to remote computers as well. Here, you use the –ComputerName parameter of these cmdlets, the cmdlets connect to the remote machine over Distributed COM (DCOM), and return the results to the local machine. For example, when you use the –ComputerName parameter of Get-Process to examine processes on remote computers, Get-Process communicates with the remote computers using DCOM and not the standard PowerShell remoting features. The exception is for session-related commands, as well as Invoke-Command, which always use either an implicitly created session or an explicitly created session. With sessions, PowerShell remoting works as discussed in this section.

REAL WORLD   PowerShell Web Access is a feature of Windows Server 2012 and later. Although you'll hear that PowerShell Web Access allows you to connect to a remote computer through a web browser, technically, that isn't

---

accurate. With PowerShell Web Access, you establish a connection to a remote server using the URI address of its HTTP or HTTPS endpoint. These connections are made over the standard TCP ports for web traffic, which by default are port 80 for HTTP and port 443 for HTTPS, but they are not established using a web browser.

Remoting Fundamentals

When you use the –ComputerName parameter of many cmdlets, the cmdlets connect to the remote machine over Distributed COM (DCOM). As DCOM uses RPC calls on dynamic ports, you may not be able to manage remote computers through firewalls. For example, when trying to work remotely through a firewall that isn't configured to allow DCOM traffic, you will get an "RPC server is not available" error and won't be able to connect. Although an administrator could configure a firewall to allow this traffic, this typically requires using a less secure configuration.

In contrast, the standard PowerShell remoting features use the WS-Management (WSMan) protocol and the Windows Remote Management (WinRM) service. When you use WSMan, PowerShell remoting connects your local PowerShell session with a PowerShell session on a remote computer. Commands you enter in the local session are sent to the remote computer, executed locally on the remote computer, and then the results are returned to your local PowerShell session. As everything runs within the same framework, you can be certain that you can consistently work with remote computers as long as you know how to establish remote sessions using PowerShell.

PowerShell remoting has significant advantages over using standard applications for remote management. One advantage is that a single TCP port is used for all standard communications and a single TCP port is used for all secure communications, which by default are ports 5985 and 5986 respectively. Thus, when you are connecting to remote computers through firewalls, only these TCP ports need to be open to establish connections. Another significant advantage is that from a single console you can simultaneously work with multiple remote computers. To do this, you simply establish a session with the computers you want to work with and then execute commands within the context of that session.

Configuring Remoting

WinRM must be configured appropriately on any computer that you want to manage remotely. You can verify the availability of WinRM and configure PowerShell for remoting via WinRM by following these steps:

1. Start Windows PowerShell as an administrator by right-clicking the Windows PowerShell shortcut and selecting Run As Administrator.

2. The WinRM service is configured for manual startup by default. You must change the startup type to Automatic and start the service on each computer you want to work with. At the PowerShell prompt, you can verify that the WinRM service is running using the following command:

```
get-service winrm
```

As shown in the following example, the value of the Status property in the output should be Running:

```
Status    Name              DisplayName
------    ----              -----------
Running   WinRM             Windows Remote Management
```

3. To configure Windows PowerShell for remoting via WinRM, type the following command:

```
Enable-PSRemoting -force
```

You can use Test-WsMan to verify that a remote computer is configured correctly and determine the version of WSMan available.

Connecting Between Domains and in Workgroups

In many cases, you will be able to work with remote computers in other domains. However, if the remote computer is not in a trusted domain, the remote computer might not be able to authenticate your credentials. To enable authentication, you need to add the remote computer to the list of trusted hosts for the local computer in WinRM.

You have several options for modifying the list of trusted hosts. The first option is to use the WinRM command-line utility and replace the existing list of trusted hosts with the value you specify using the following syntax

```
winrm s winrm/config/client
'@{TrustedHosts="RemoteComputer"}'
```

where RemoteComputer is the name or IP address of the remote computer, such as

```
winrm s winrm/config/client
'@{TrustedHosts="CorpServer56"}'
```

Or

```
winrm s winrm/config/client
'@{TrustedHosts="192.168.10.80"}'
```

To confirm that the computer was added to the TrustHosts list, display the WinRM client configuration details by entering: **winrm g winrm/config/client**.

Another way to specify a remote host to trust is to use Set-Item and the WSMan: provider to modify the TrustedHosts list. Unlike the WinRM utility, which replaces the trusted hosts list, the WSMan: provider adds the value you specify to the existing list, making it easier for you to specify multiple trusted hosts. The basic syntax is:

```
Set-Item -Path WSMan:\localhost\Client\TrustedHosts
-Value 'RemoteComputer'
```

where RemoteComputer is the name of the remote computer, such as

```
Set-Item -Path WSMan:\localhost\Client\TrustedHosts
-Value 'MailServer12'
```

> **NOTE**   Typically, you are prompted to confirm that you want to modify the TrustedHosts lists. Confirm that you do by pressing Y. To bypass this message, use the –Force parameter. Note also that you can set values in this way because the WSMan: provider adds the value to the existing value by setting –Concatenate to $true automatically.

If you're wondering which hosts are trusted, you can list trusted hosts by entering:

```
Get-Item -Path WSMan:\localhost\Client\TrustedHosts |fl
name, value
```

When you are working with computers in workgroups, accessing a domain computer from a workgroup or vice versa, you must either use HTTPS as the transport or add the remote machine to the TrustedHosts configuration settings. If you cannot connect to a remote host, verify that the service on the remote host is running and is accepting requests by running the following command on the remote host:

```
winrm quickconfig
```

This command analyzes and configures the WinRM service. If the WinRM service is set up correctly, you'll see output similar to the following:

```
WinRM service is already running on this machine.
WinRM is already set up for remote management on this
computer.
```

If the WinRM service is not set up correctly, you see output similar to the following and need to respond affirmatively to several prompts. When this process completes, WinRM should be set up correctly.

```
WinRM Quick Configuration
Running command "Set-WSManQuickConfig" to enable remote
management of this computer by using the Windows Remote
Management (WinRM) service.
 This includes:
1. Starting or restarting (if already started) the WinRM
service
2. Setting the WinRM service startup type to Automatic
3. Creating a listener to accept requests on any IP
address
4. Enabling Windows Firewall inbound rule exceptions for
WS-Management traffic (for http only).
```

```
Do you want to continue?
[Y] Yes   [A] Yes to All   [N] No   [L] No to All   [S]
Suspend   [?] Help (default is "Y"): Y
WinRM has been updated to receive requests.
WinRM service type changed successfully.

WinRM has been updated for remote management.
Created a WinRM listener on HTTP://* to accept WS-Man
requests to any IP on this machine.
WinRM firewall exception enabled.

Confirm
Are you sure you want to perform this action?
Performing the operation "Set-PSSessionConfiguration" on
target "Name: microsoft.powershell SDDL:
O:NSG:BAD:P(A;;GA;;;BA)(A;;GA;;;RM)S:P(AU;FA;GA;;;WD)(AU;
SA;GXGW;;;WD). This lets selected users remotely run
Windows
PowerShell commands on this computer.".
[Y] Yes   [A] Yes to All   [N] No   [L] No to All   [S]
Suspend   [?] Help (default is "Y"): Y
```

Creating HTTPS and Other Listeners

By default, WinRM QuickConfig creates an HTTP listener on a
remote host, but does not create an HTTPS listener. If you want
to make HTTPS connections to the remote host, you'll do the
following:

1. Obtain an SSL certificate for the remote computer and
make sure the certificate has common name (CN) entry that
matches the identifier you are using.

2. Install the remote computer's SSL certificate in the
certificate store for the management computer you are using
(and not the user's certificate store).

3. On the remote computer, use New-WSManInstance to add an HTTPS listener for WSMan.

To create an HTTPS listener for WSMan, you need the thumbprint value of the remote computer's SSL certificate. One way to obtain this value is to access the Cert: provider and list the certificate thumbprints, as shown in this example:

```
Get-ChildItem -Path cert:\LocalMachine -Recurse |
select Subject, FriendlyName, Thumbprint | fl
```

After you obtain the certificate thumbprint, you can use New-WSManInstance to create the HTTPS listener on the remote computer, such as:

```
$thumbprint = "XXX-XXXX-XX-XXXX-XX"
New-WSManInstance -ResourceURI winrm/config/Listener
-SelectorSet @{Transport='HTTPS',
Address="IP:192.168.10.34"}
-ValueSet @{Hostname="Server12.Imaginedlands.com",
CertificateThumbprint=$thumprint}
```

Here, you create an HTTPS listener for Server12. As mentioned previously, WinRM listens on port 5985 for HTTP and port 5986 for HTTPS. Although you can configure alternate listening ports, you must delete the current listening port before creating a new listening port, as shown in this example:

```
winrm delete
winrm/config/listener?Address=*+Transport=HTTP

winrm create
winrm/config/listener?Address=*+Transport=HTTP
@{Port="5999"}
```

> **NOTE** As the port change applies to all computers and sessions the computer runs, you should only change the listening port if required by IT policy or firewall settings.

Generally, to use PowerShell remoting features, you must start Windows PowerShell as an administrator by right-clicking the Windows PowerShell shortcut and selecting Run As Administrator. When starting PowerShell from another program, such as the command prompt (cmd.exe), you must start that program as an administrator.

9. Executing Remote Commands

You can use Windows PowerShell remoting to run cmdlets and external programs on remote computers. For example, you can run any built-in cmdlets and external programs accessible in the PATH environment variable ($env:path). However, because PowerShell runs as a network service or local service, you cannot use PowerShell to open the user interface for any program on a remote computer. If you try to start a program with a graphical interface, the program process starts but the command cannot complete, and the PowerShell prompt does not return until the program is finished or you press Ctrl+C.

Understanding Remote Execution

When you submit a remote command, the command is transmitted across the network to the Windows PowerShell client on the designated remote computer, and runs in the Windows PowerShell client on the remote computer. The command results are sent back to the local computer and appear in the Windows PowerShell session on the local computer. Note that all of the local input to a remote command is collected before being sent to the remote computer, but the output is returned to the local computer as it is generated.

Whenever you use PowerShell remoting features, keep the following in mind:

- You must start Windows PowerShell as an administrator by right-clicking the Windows PowerShell shortcut and selecting Run As Administrator. When starting PowerShell from another program, such as the command prompt (cmd.exe), you must start that program as an administrator.

▪ The current user must be a member of the Administrators group on the remote computer or be able to provide the credentials of an administrator. When you connect to a remote computer, PowerShell uses your user name and password credentials to log on to the remote computer. The credentials are encrypted.

▪ When you work remotely, you use multiple instances of Windows PowerShell: a local instance and one or more remote instances. Generally, in the local instance, the policies and profiles on the local computer are in effect. On a remote instance, the policies and profiles on the remote computer are in effect. This means cmdlets, aliases, functions, preferences, and other elements in the local profile are not necessarily available to remote commands. To ensure you can use cmdlets, aliases, functions, preferences, and other elements in the local profile with remote commands, you must copy the local profiles to each remote computer.

▪ Although you can execute commands on remote computers, any files, directories, and additional resources that are needed to execute a command must exist on the remote computer. Additionally, your user account must have permission to connect to the remote computer, permission to run Windows PowerShell, and permission to access files, directories, and other resources on the remote computer.

▪ The functionality available through your remote session depends on the version of PowerShell on the remote computer. For example, if you connect to a remote computer that has PowerShell 3.0 installed, you cannot use the features of PowerShell 4.0, even if PowerShell 4.0 is available on your local machine.

Standard Commands for Remoting

Except when you are using CIM sessions, the cmdlets you'll use for remoting include:

- **Connect-PSSession** Reconnects to one or more PowerShell sessions that were disconnected. You can use Connect-PSSession to connect to any valid disconnected session, including those that were started in other sessions or on other computers, those that were disconnected intentionally, such as by using the Disconnect-PSSession cmdlet, and that were disconnected unintentionally, such as by a network interruption when running the Invoke-Command cmdlet. Session objects are instantiated when you create a session in the PowerShell console or the PowerShell application. A session object is created for each remote computer to which you connect. As long as the session objects are valid and you have appropriate credentials, you can use these objects to reconnect to the sessions.

- **Disconnect-PSSession** Disconnects a PowerShell session. You can only disconnect from open non-interactive sessions, meaning you can disconnect from sessions started with New-PSSession but cannot disconnect from sessions started with Enter-PSSession. Additionally, you cannot disconnect from closed or broken sessions.

- **Enter-PSSession** Starts an interactive session with a single remote computer. During the session, you can run commands just as if you were typing directly on the remote computer. You can have only one interactive session at a time. Typically, you use the –ComputerName parameter to specify the name of the remote computer. However, you can also use a session that you created previously by using New-PSSession for the interactive session.

- **Exit-PSSession**   Ends an interactive session and disconnects from the remote computer. You can also type **exit** to end an interactive session. The effect is the same as using Exit-PSSession.

- **Export-PSSession**   Gets cmdlets, functions, aliases, and other command types from an open session and saves them in a Windows PowerShell script module file (.psm1). When you want to use the commands from the script module, use the Add-Module cmdlet to add the commands to the local session so that they can be used. To export commands, first use New-PSSession to connect to the session that has the commands that you want to export. Then use Export-PSSession to export the commands. By default, Export-PSSession exports all commands except for commands that already exist in the session. However, you can use the –PSSnapin, –CommandName, and –CommandType parameters to specify the commands to export.

- **Get-PSSession**   Gets the PowerShell sessions (PSSessions) that were created in the current session. Without parameters, this cmdlet returns all available PSSessions. You can use the parameters of Get-PSSession to get the sessions that are connected to particular computers or identify sessions by their names, IDs, or instance IDs. For computers, type the NetBIOS name, IP address, or fully qualified domain name. To specify the local computer, enter the computer name, localhost, or a dot (.). For IDs, type an integer value that uniquely identifies the PSSession in the current session. PSSessions can be assigned friendly names with the –Name parameter. You can reference the friendly names using wildcards. To find the names and IDs of PSSessions, use Get-PSSession without parameters. An instance ID is a GUID that uniquely identifies a PSSession, even when you have multiple sessions running in PowerShell. The instance ID is stored in the RemoteRunspaceID property of the RemoteRunspaceInfo object that represents a PSSession. To find the InstanceID of the PSSessions in the current session, enter **get-pssession | Format-Table Name, ComputerName, RemoteRunspaceId**.

- **Import-PSSession** Imports cmdlets, aliases, functions, and other command types from an open session into the current session on your management computer. You can import any command that Get-Command can find in the other session. To import commands, first use New-PSSession to connect to the session from which you will import. Then use Import-PSSession to import commands. By default, Import-PSSession imports all commands except for commands that exist in the current session. To overwrite existing commands, use the –AllowClobber parameter. PowerShell adds the imported commands to a temporary module that exists only in your session, and it returns an object that represents the module. Although you can use imported commands just as you would use any command in the session, the imported part of the command actually runs in the session from which it was imported. Because imported commands might take longer to run than local commands, Import-PSSession adds an –AsJob parameter to every imported command. This parameter allows you to run the command as a PowerShell background job.

- **Invoke-Command** Runs commands on a local computer or one or more remote computers, and returns all output from the commands, including errors. Use the –ComputerName parameter to run a single command on a remote computer. To run a series of related commands that share data, create a PowerShell session (PSSession) on a remote computer, and then use the –Session parameter of Invoke-Command to run the command in the PSSession or use the –InDisconnectedSession parameter to run commands without maintaining persistent connections to the remote sessions.

▪ **New-PSSession**   Creates a PowerShell session (PSSession) on a local or remote computer. When you create a PSSession, Windows PowerShell establishes a persistent connection to the remote computer, and you can use the PSSession to interact directly with the computer.

▪ **Receive-PSSession**   Gets the results of commands running in PowerShell sessions that were disconnected. Receive-PSSession connects to the session, resumes any commands that were suspended, and gets the results of commands running in the session. You can use a Receive-PSSession in addition to or in place of a Connect-PSSession command. Receive-PSSession can connect to any disconnected or reconnected session, including those that were started in other sessions or on other computers, those that were disconnected intentionally, such as by using the Disconnect-PSSession cmdlet, and that were disconnected unintentionally, such as by a network interruption when running the Invoke-Command cmdlet. If you use the Receive-PSSession cmdlet to connect to a session in which no commands are running or suspended, Receive-PSSession connects to the session, but returns no output or errors.

▪ **Remove-PSSession**   Closes one or more PowerShell sessions and frees the resources the sessions were using. It is a best practice to remove sessions when you are finished using them.

Invoking Remote Commands

One way to run commands on remote computers is to use the Invoke-Command cmdlet. With this cmdlet, you can do the following:

- Run commands in an implicitly-created PowerShell session, in an explicitly-created PowerShell session, in a disconnected session, or as a background job.
- Use the –ComputerName parameter to specify the remote computers to work with by DNS name, NetBIOS name, or IP address.
- When working with multiple remote computers, separate each computer name or IP address with a comma.
- Enclose your command or commands to execute in curly braces, which denotes a script block, and use the –ScriptBlock parameter to specify the command or commands to run.

For example, you can type the following command as a single line to run a Get-Process command remotely:

```
invoke-command -computername Server43, Server27, Server82
-scriptblock {get-process}
```

Here, you are opening temporary sessions to Server43, Server27 and Server82, and running the Get-Process command. The results from the command execution on each remote computer are returned as results to the local computer. If the temporary session is interrupted, such as by a network or power outage, PowerShell creates a background job for the disconnected session, which makes it easier to reconnect, resume execution and get the results.

> **MORE INFO**   Although you are using an implicitly created session, the session works much like a standard PowerShell session. As discussed in "Navigating Remote Connection Issues," in Chapter 10 later in this text, this means PowerShell connects over WSMan, the results are serialized using XML, and passed over WSMan back to the local machine where the results are deserialized.
>
> By default, Invoke-Command runs under your user name and credentials. Use the –Credential parameter to specify alternate credentials using the UserName or Domain\UserName syntax. You will be prompted for a password.
>
> **REAL WORLD**   When you connect to a remote computer that is running Windows or Windows Server, the default starting location is the home directory of the current user, which is stored in the %HomePath% environment variable ($env:homepath) and the Windows PowerShell $home variable.

When you use Invoke-Command, the cmdlet returns an object that includes the name of the computer that generated the data. The remote computer name is stored in the PSComputerName property. Typically, the PSComputerName property is displayed by default. You can use the –HideComputerName parameter to hide the PSComputerName property.

If the PSComputerName property isn't displayed and you want to see the source computer name, use the Format-Table cmdlet to add the PSComputerName property to the output as shown in the following example:

```
$procs = invoke-command -script {get-process | sort-
object -property Name} -computername Server56, Server42,
Server27

&$procs | format-table Name, Handles, WS, CPU,
PSComputerName -auto
```

```
Name             Handles   WS         CPU PSComputerName
----             -------   --         --- --------------
acrotray              52   3948544      0 Server56
AlertService         139   7532544        Server56
csrss                594   20463616       Server56
csrss                655   5283840        Server56
CtHelper              96   6705152 0.078125 Server56

acrotray              43   3948234      0 Server42
AlertService         136   7532244        Server42
csrss                528   20463755       Server42
csrss                644   5283567        Server42
CtHelper              95   6705576 0.067885 Server42

acrotray              55   3967544      0 Server27
AlertService         141   7566662        Server27
csrss                590   20434342       Server27
csrss                654   5242340        Server27
CtHelper              92   6705231 0.055522 Server27
```

> **NOTE** It's important to point out that because the object is serialized and deserialized, the object's methods aren't available. Although this happens across any WSMan connection, this doesn't happen when DCOM is used.

PowerShell includes a per-command throttling feature that lets you limit the number of concurrent remote connections that are established for a command. Generally, the default is 32 or 50 concurrent connections, depending on the cmdlet. You can use the –ThrottleLimit parameter to set a custom throttle limit for a command. Keep in mind the throttling feature is applied to each command, not to the entire session or to the computer. If you are running a command concurrently in several sessions, the number of concurrent connections is the sum of the concurrent connections in all sessions.

Keep in mind that although PowerShell can manage hundreds of concurrent remote connections, the number of remote commands that you can send might be limited by the resources of your computer and its ability to establish and maintain multiple network connections. To add more protection for remoting, you can use the –UseSSL parameter of Invoke-Command. As with commands that are run locally, you can pause or terminate a remote command by pressing Ctrl+S or Ctrl+C.

REAL WORLD PowerShell remoting is available even when the local computer is not in a domain. For testing and development, you can use the remoting features to connect to and create sessions on the same computer. PowerShell remoting works the same as when you are connecting to a remote computer.

To run remote commands on a computer in a workgroup, you might need to change Windows security settings on the management and target computers. On the target computer, meaning to which you want to connect, you must allow remote access to the computer using Enable-PSRemoting – Force. On your management computer, meaning the computer you are working from, you must either run Enable-PSRemoting or do the following: ensure the WinRM service is started and enable the local account token filter policy by ensuring the LocalAccountTokenFilterPolicy registry entry in

---

HKLM\SOFTWARE\Microsoft\Windows\CurrentVersion\Polici es\System has its value set to 1.

You can determine whether the WinRM service is running by entering **Get-Service WinRM**. You can check the version of WinRM that's installed by entering **Test-WSMan –Auth default**. Enter **Get-PSSessionConfiguration** to check the remoting configuration for PowerShell.

10. Managing PowerShell Sessions

Windows PowerShell supports both local and remote sessions. A *session* is a runspace that establishes a common working environment for commands. Commands in a session can share data. After you create a session, you can work with it interactively by using Enter-PSSession or you can invoke commands against the session by using Invoke-Command. When you are finished using a session, you can disconnect from it and reconnect later or you can exit the session to free up the resources used by the session.

Invoking Sessions

Using the New-PSSession cmdlet, you can establish a session to create a persistent connection to a computer you want to work with. Unless you use the –ComputerName parameter and use it to specify the name of one or more remote computers, PowerShell assumes you are creating a session for the local computer. With New-PSSession, you must use the –Session parameter with Invoke-Command to run the command in the named session. For example, you can establish a session by typing the following command:

```
$s = New-PSSession –ComputerName Server24
```

Here, *$s* is a variable that stores the session object. PowerShell knows you are creating a remote session because you've used the –ComputerName parameter. PowerShell creates a persistent connection with the specified computer. Use Invoke-Command with the –Session parameter to run the command in the named session as shown in this example:

```
invoke-command -session $s -scriptblock {get-process}
```

Here, you use Invoke-Command to run Get-Process in the $s session. Because this session is connected to a remote computer, the command runs on the remote computer.

When you create a session, you can control the session via the session object that is returned. If you want to get information about remote sessions on a particular remote computer, you can use Get-PSSession. For example, you could enter **get-pssession –ComputerName Server24 | fl**. You'd then see detailed information about remote sessions on this computer and their status, such as:

```
ComputerName            : CorpServer134
ConfigurationName       : Microsoft.PowerShell
InstanceId              :
Id                      : 2
Name                    : IT
Availability            : Available
ApplicationPrivateData  : {DebugMode, DebugStop,
PSVersionTable, DebugBreakpointCount}
Runspace        :
System.Management.Automation.RemoteRunspace
State                   : Opened
IdleTimeout             : 7200000
OutputBufferingMode     : Block
DisconnectedOn          :
ExpiresOn               :
```

As you can see from the output, the session is assigned the session ID of 2. This ID also can be used to work with or get information about the session. For example, if you enter **get-pssession –id 2 | fl** you'd get the same information.

> **NOTE** Sessions also can be controlled via a name assigned when invoking the session. Use the –Name parameter to set

the name. If you don't specify a name for the session, a default name typically is assigned, based on the ID of the session. For example, if the session ID is 11, the automatically assigned name typically is Session11.

The output of Get-PSSession provides additional information that is useful for working with sessions, including:

- **ConfigurationName**   Specifies the type of session, which is important for differentiating PowerShell sessions and CIM sessions. PowerShell sessions are listed as Microsoft.PowerShell.
- **Availability**   Specifies the availability of the session with respect to the current PowerShell window. A session listed as Available was created in the current window. A session listed with another value wasn't created in the current window. Generally, None means the session is not available and Busy means the session is active in another window or on another computer.
- **State**   Specifies the state of the session. A session listed as Opened was created in the current window and is active. A session listed as Broken was unintentionally disconnected. A session listed as Disconnected was intentionally disconnected.

Although the examples so far work with one computer, you can just as easily establish a session with multiple computers. Simply establish the session and name all the computers in a comma-separated list, such as:

```
$s = New-PSSession -ComputerName Server24, Server37,
Server92
```

By default, your current credentials are used to establish connections. However, you might also need to specify a user account that has permissions to perform remote administration using the –Credential parameter.

You can provide alternative credentials in one of two ways. You can:

- Pass in a Credential object to provide the information required for authentication. A Credential object has UserName and Password properties. Although the user name is stored as a regular string, the password is stored as a secure, encrypted string.
- Specify the user account that has permission to perform the action. After you specify a user name, PowerShell displays a prompt for the user's password. When prompted, enter the password and then click OK.

> **REAL WORLD**   With credentials, the user name can be provided in several formats. If you are working in a domain and the appropriate domain is already shown in the credentials dialog box, you don't have to specify the domain as part of the user name. However, if you are working in a domain and the domain isn't set, you should provide the required domain and user information using the Domain\UserName format, such as ImaginedL\WilliamS for the user WilliamS working in the ImaginedL domain. Additionally, if you want to work with a local computer account rather than a domain account, you can specify a local computer account using the ComputerName\UserName format, such as PC29\TomG for the local user TomG on PC29.

To see how the –Credential parameter can be used, consider the following example:

```
$t = New-PSSession -ComputerName Server24, Server45,
Server36 -Credential Cpandl\WilliamS
```

Here, you establish a session with Server24, Server45, and
Server36 and specify your domain and user name. As a result,
when you use Invoke-Command to run commands in the $t
session, the commands run on each remote computer with
those credentials. Note that although this is a single session,
each runspace on each computer is separate.

Extending this idea, you can also just as easily get the list of
remote computers from a text file. In this example, servers.txt
contains a comma-separated list of computers:

```
$ses = get-content c:\test\servers.txt | new-pssession
-credential cpandl\williams
```

Here, the contents of the Servers.txt file are piped to New-
PSSession. As a result, the $ses session is established with all
computers listed in the file. Typically, the names are provided in
a comma-separate list, such as:

```
Server14, Server87, Server21
```

Sometimes, you'll want to execute an application or external
utility on a remote computer as shown in the following example:

```
$comp = get-content c:\computers.txt
$s = new-pssession -computername $comp
invoke-command -session $s { powercfg.exe -energy }
```

Here, C:\Computers.txt is the path to the file containing the list
of remote computers to check. On each computer, you run
PowerCfg with the –Energy parameter. This generates an
Energy-Report.html file in the default directory for the user

account used to access the computer. The energy report provides details on power configuration settings and issues that are causing power management not to work correctly. If you'd rather not have to retrieve the report from each computer, you can write the report to a share and base the report name on the computer name, as shown in the following example:

```
$comp = get-content c:\computers.txt
$s = new-pssession -computername $comp
invoke-command -session $s { powercfg.exe -energy -output
"\\fileserver72\reports\$env:computername.html"}
```

Here, you write the report to the \\fileserver72\reports share and name the file using the value of the ComputerName environment variable. Note that when you work with PowerShell and are referencing applications and external utilities, you must specify the .exe file extension with the program name.

When you are running commands on many remote computers, you might not want to wait for the commands to return before performing other tasks. To avoid having to wait, use Invoke-Command with the –AsJob parameter to create a background job in each of the runspaces:

```
invoke-command -session $s -scriptblock {get-process
moddr | stop-process -force } -AsJob
```

Here, you use Invoke-Command to get and stop a named process via the $s session. Because the command is run as a background job, the prompt returns immediately without waiting for the command to run on each computer.

Although being able to establish a session on many computers is handy, sometimes you might want to work interactively with a single remote computer. To do this, you can use the Enter-

PSSession cmdlet to start an interactive session with a remote computer. At the Windows Powershell prompt, type **Enter-PSSession *ComputerName***, where *ComputerName* is the name of the remote computer. The command prompt changes to show that you are connected to the remote computer, as shown in the following example:

```
[Server49]: PS C:\Users\wrstanek.cpandl\Documents>
```

Now the commands that you type run on the remote computer just as if you had typed them directly on the remote computer. For enhanced security through encryption of transmissions, the Enter-PSSession cmdlet also supports the –Credential and –UseSSL parameters. You can end the interactive session using the command Exit-PSSession or by typing **exit**.

Navigating Remote Connection Issues

When you are working with remote computers, you need to keep in mind the following:

- How commands are executed
- How objects are serialized

Whether you use Invoke-Command or Enter-PSSession with remote computers, Windows PowerShell establishes a temporary connection, uses the connection to run the current command, and then closes the connection each time you run a command. This is an efficient method for running a single command or several unrelated commands, even on a large number of remote computers.

The New-PSSession cmdlet provides an alternative by establishing a session with a persistent connection. With New-PSSession, Windows PowerShell establishes a persistent connection and uses the connection to run any commands you enter. Because you can run multiple commands in a single, persistent runspace, the commands can share data, including the values of variables, the definitions of aliases, and the contents of functions. New-PSSession also supports the –UseSSL parameter.

When you use Windows PowerShell locally, you work with live .NET Framework objects, and these objects are associated with actual programs or components. When you invoke the methods or change the properties of live objects, the changes affect the actual program or component. And, when the properties of a program or component change, the properties of the object that represent them change too.

Because live objects cannot be transmitted over the network, Windows PowerShell serializes the objects sent in remote commands. This means it converts each object into a series of Constraint Language in XML (CLiXML) data elements for transmission. When Windows PowerShell receives a serialized file, it converts the XML into a deserialized object type. Although the deserialized object is an accurate record of the properties of the program or component at execution time, it is no longer directly associated with the originating component, and the methods are removed because they are no longer effective. Also, the serialized objects returned by the Invoke-Command cmdlet have additional properties that help you determine the origin of the command.

> **NOTE** You can use Export-Clixml to create XML-based representations of objects and store them in a file. The objects stored in the file are serialized. To import a CLiXML file and create deserialized objects, you can use Import-CLixml.

Disconnecting Sessions

With PowerShell 3.0 and later, sessions can be disconnected and reconnected. Although a power loss or temporary network outage can unintentionally disconnect you from a session, you disconnect from a session intentionally by using Disconnect-PSSession. Alternatively, you can run Invoke-Command with the –InDisconnectedSession parameter to run commands in a disconnected state.

When you disconnect from a session, any command or scripts that are running in the session continue running, and you can later reconnect to the session to pick up where you left off. You also can reconnect to a session if you were disconnected unintentionally.

Because you can only disconnect from open non-interactive sessions, you can disconnect from sessions started with New-PSSession, but cannot disconnect from sessions started with Enter-PSSession. Also, you cannot disconnect from closed or broken sessions, or sessions started in other PowerShell windows or by other users.

You can disconnect a session using its object, its ID or its name. In the following example, you create a session, work with the remote computer and then disconnect from the session:

```
$s = new-pssession -computername corpserver74
invoke-command -session $s { get-process }
```

. . .

```
disconnect-pssession -session $s
```

You can only disconnect sessions that are in the Opened state.
To disconnect all open sessions at the same time, enter the
following command:

```
Get-PSSession | Disconnect-PSSession
```

As you can't disconnect sessions that are already disconnected
or broken, PowerShell will display errors if any sessions are in
these states. To avoid these errors, you can use a filter to specify
that you only want to disconnect Opened sessions. Here is an
example:

```
get-pssession | where {$_.state -eq "Opened"} |
disconnect-pssession
```

Here, Get-PSSession lists all current sessions and then you filter
the output using the Where-Object cmdlet so that only sessions
with the State property set to Opened are passed through the
pipeline and disconnected.

Sessions are considered to be idle when they are disconnected,
even if commands are running. By default, sessions can be idle
for 7200000 milliseconds (2 hours) before they are closed. Use –
IdleTimeoutSec to specify a different timeout, up to 12 hours. In
the following example, the time out is set to 8 hours (60
seconds x 60 x 8):

```
disconnect-pssession -session $s -idletimeout 60*60*8
```

> **REAL WORLD**   The output buffering mode determines whether commands continue to run while a session is disconnected. The default output buffering mode for disconnected sessions is Block, which means command execution is suspended when the output buffer fills and doesn't resume again until the session is reconnected. Alternatively, you can set the output buffering mode to Drop, which ensures that commands keep executing when the output buffer fills. However, with Drop, as new output is saved, the oldest output is discarded by default. To prevent this, redirect the command output to a file.

Reconnecting Sessions

To connect to any disconnected session, including those that were started in other sessions or on other computers, those that were disconnected intentionally, and those that were disconnected unintentionally, you have several choices. You can use either Connect-PSSession or Receive-PSSession.

The difference between connecting to a session and receiving a session is subtle but important. When you connect to a session, you reconnect to the session and are able to begin working with the remote computer or computers to which the session connects. When you receive a connection, you reconnect to the session, resume any commands that were suspended, and get the results of commands running in the session.

Whether you are reconnecting to a session using Connect-PSSession or Receive-PSSession, you need to identify the session to which you want to connect. If you are using the same computer and the same PowerShell window, you can enter **Get-**

PSSession to list sessions by ID and name and then reconnect to sessions, as shown in the following examples:

```
connect-pssession -session $s
connect-pssession -id 2
connect-pssession -name CheckServerTasks
```

If you are using a different computer or PowerShell window, you'll need to use the –ComputerName parameter with Get-PSSession to list sessions on remote computers and then reconnect to sessions. Consider the following example and sample output:

```
Get-PSSession -ComputerName Server24, Server45, Server36
-Credential Cpandl\WilliamS
```

Id	Name	ComputerName	State	ConfigurationName	Availability
2	Task	Server24	Disconnected	Microsoft.PowerShell	None
3	Session12	Server45	Opened	Microsoft.PowerShell	Available
4	Clnr	Server36	Broken	Microsoft.PowerShell	None
5	SChks	Server36	Disconnected	Microsoft.PowerShell	Busy

Here, you find that each of the servers has active sessions. Although the session IDs are generated on a one up basis on the local computer, the session names are the actual names assigned either automatically or by users when the sessions were created. Note also that ComputerName identifies the remote computer and State specifies the state of the session as being Opened, Disconnected or Broken. Opened connections are already active in the current window.

You can reconnect disconnected and broken sessions, provided the sessions aren't active (busy). However, be sure to connect using the name assigned rather than the locally generated ID.

For example, you could use the following command to reconnect to the Task session on Server24:

```
connect-pssession -computername server24 -name task
```

However, you could not use the locally generated session ID to connect to the Task session. Why? Because the session ID is locally generated and does not match the session ID on Server74.

PowerShell also allows you to reconnect multiple sessions simultaneously. Consider the following example and sample output:

```
Get-PSSession -ComputerName Server74, Server38, Server45
-Credential Cpandl\WilliamS

Id Name      ComputerName  State        ConfigurationName    Availability
-- ----      ------------  -----        -----------------    ------------
8 Session14 Server74 Disconnected Microsoft.PowerShell       None
9 Session18 Server38 Broken       Microsoft.PowerShell       None
10 SChks    Server45     Disconnected Microsoft.PowerShell    None
```

Here, you have sessions on three different servers that are available to be connected. If you wanted to reconnect the sessions to continue working with the servers, the easiest way to do this would be to enter:

```
Get-PSSession -ComputerName Server74, Server38, Server45
-Credential Cpandl\WilliamS | Connect-PSSession
```

Or

```
$s = Get-PSSession -ComputerName Server74, Server38,
Server45 -Credential Cpandl\WilliamS | Connect-PSSession
```

Here, you get the sessions that were created on the remote computers and use Connect-PSSession to reconnect the sessions.

> **NOTE** Connect-PSSession has no effect on valid, active sessions. If the servers had sessions that were opened or disconnected but busy, those sessions would not be reconnected.

Once you've reconnected sessions, the sessions can be accessed in the current PowerShell window by ID and name. If you didn't assign the sessions to variables directly, you'll need to do so before you can work with the sessions using Invoke-Command. Enter **Get-PSSession** to get information about the sessions, and then use the (valid) locally assigned ID or the session name to assign sessions to a session variable, such as:

```
$session = get-pssession -id 2, 3, 12
```

Here, you store the session objects for the sessions with the local ID of 2, 3, and 12 in the $session variable. You can then use the $session variable to pass commands to all three remote computers, such as:

```
$session = get-pssession -id 2, 3, 12

invoke-command -session $session { get-eventlog system |
where {$_.entrytype -eq "Error"} }
```

When you are completely finished with a session, you should use Remove-PSSession to remove it. Removing a session stops any commands or scripts that are running, ends the session, and releases the resources the session was using.

Contents in Review

Active Directory

2nd Edition

Fast
Start

Your Quick Start Guide for Active Directory.

Smart Brain
Training Solutions

Exchange Online

2nd Edition

Fast Start

Your Quick Start Guide for Exchange Online, Office 365 and Windows Azure

Smart Brain
Training Solutions

www.ingramcontent.com/pod-product-compliance
Lightning Source LLC
Chambersburg PA
CBHW071213050326
40689CB00011B/2316